How to Get
More from Your
Satnav

R T Scanlon

authorHOUSE®

AuthorHouse™
1663 Liberty Drive
Bloomington, IN 47403
www.authorhouse.com
Phone: 1-800-839-8640

RENFREWSHIRE COUNCIL		
186599721		
Bertrams	29/07/2013	
	£9.95	
ERS		

Published by AuthorHouse   05/29/2013

ISBN: 978-1-4772-1920-1 (sc)
ISBN: 978-1-4772-1921-8 (e)

CONTENTS

Lists of Charts, Figures, and Tables.. vii

Acknowledgements.. ix

Foreword.. xiii

Introduction..xv

Chapter 1: Literature Search... 1

Chapter 2: Difficulties Associated with Inputting an
            Address or Postcode...................................... 29

Chapter 3: Route Planning: How to Be More
            Effective Than Satnav.................................... 47

Chapter 4: Using a Satnav while Driving........................... 71

Chapter 5: Review of a High-specification Satnav with
            Live Traffic Updates..................................... 79

Chapter 6: Evaluation of the Satnav Concept...................... 85

Conclusion... 95

Appendices.. 103

References 105

Additional Notes 107

Index... 109

LISTS OF CHARTS,
FIGURES, AND TABLES

List of charts

1. How to develop skill with a satnav. xvi
2. Links in the chain of communication
    when confirming a destination. 36
3. Understanding where errors occur. 39
4. How to verify a destination as correct when a
    postcode is input for the UK. 42
5. How to verify a destination as correct
    when an address is used (UK and USA) 43
6. How to verify a destination as correct
    when an atlas is used (UK and USA). 44
7. Some of the TomTom menu options
    that allow you to take control. 100

List of figures

1. How satnav plans routes. 54
2. A 'best-fit,' satnav-generated route. 54
3. An alternative 'best-fit,' satnav-generated route. 55
4. Routes not likely to be planned by satnav. 56
5. The alternative major road technique. 57
6. A satnav route prior to planning the backflip. 58
7. User-adjusted route the backflip. 59
8. Satnav route before planning the slingshot. 60
9. How to plan the slingshot. 60
10. Satnav route before planning the reverse slingshot. 61
11. User-adjusted route; the slingshot. 61

12. Correcting an excessively long satnav route. 64
13. How to turn off route to avoid congestion. 73
14. How to avoid congestion on a major road. 75
15. Just-In-Time (JIT) approach. 86
16. Well-Before-Time (WBT) approach. 89

List of tables

1. History of the satnav. 2
2. Survey of drivers' experiences by Direct Line. 3
3. Route planner v. satnav comparison. 9
4. Comment s on Collin's *Sat Nav Buddy*: entering data. 11
5. Comment s on Collin's *Sat Nav Buddy*:
   driving with your satnav. 13
6. Comment s on *Philip's Navigator Trucker's Britain*. 15
7. Why you should always carry a map according to
   Philip's Navigator Trucker's Britain. 16
8. Understanding postcodes in the UK. 29
9. Comparison of basic-model satnavs;
   revealing route-planning features. 48
10. Comparison of shortest- and fastest-route options. 52
11. PC software for route planning. 67
12. Smartphone apps for advanced routing 69

ACKNOWLEDGEMENTS

I wish to acknowledge, with grateful thanks, permission to quote from the following copyrighted material:

Automobile Association. Chapter 1.

- For reference to the website Route Planner. Used with permission of the Automobile Association in the United Kingdom (www. theaa.com).
- For the survey results. Used with permission of Automobile Association/Populus Poll.

Advanced Driving. Chapter 1.

- For references to Advanced Driving. Used with permission of The Institute of Advanced Motorists in the UK (www.iam.uk).

Chipperfield. Chapter 1.

- For references to *The Sunday Times* article 'The Next Satnav Revolution Is Afoot.' Used with permission of Ed Chipperfield.

Direct Line. Chapter 1.

- For reference to the survey conducted by Direct Line. Used with permission of The Royal Bank of Scotland Insurance Services, UK.

Eyre. Chapter 1.

- For reference to communication theory from E. C. Eyre. *Mastering Basic Management,* London Macmillan (1982). Used with permission of Palgrave Macmillan.

Garmin. Chapter 3.

- For reference to Garmin in the table of basic-model satnavs. Used with permission of Garmin (Europe) Ltd. (www.garimin.com).

Google. Chapter 3.

- For reference to Google map app in the table of basic-model satnavs. Used with permission of Google Maps (www.google.com/mobile/navigation).

Postcodes. Chapter 2.

- For references regarding postcode analysis. Used with permission of Not Panicking Ltd owners of the h2g2 website and also the authors of the particular website posts: written and researched by the_jon_m and edited by Lbclaire.

RoSPA. Chapter 1.

- For references to safety considerations regarding vehicle technology. Used with permission of The Royal Society for the Prevention of Accidents in the UK (www.rospa.com).

The Knowledge. Chapter 1.

- For the references to The Knowledge. Used with permission of Information, Access, and Compliance Team, Transport for London, Windsor House, 42-50 Victoria Street, London SW1H 0TL.

TomTom. Chapter 3.

- For the references to TomTom in the comparison table regarding route planning. Used with permission of TomTom International BV, The Netherlands.

Chapter 5.

- For the references to TomTom Go Live 1000 in the review of this product. Used with permission of TomTom International BV, The Netherlands.

Navman. Chapter 3.

- For the references to the basic-model Navman in the comparison table. Used with permission of Navman Automotive Business, Navman Technology, NZ Ltd, 7-11 Kavana Street, Northcote, Auckland, New Zealand.

Which? Chapter 1.

- For the references to Which? consumer advice on satnavs. Used with permission of Which?, 2 Marylebone Road, London NW1 4DF.

Chapter 3.

- For reference to the smartphone app comparison to the handheld satnav. Used with permission of Which?, 2 Marylebone Road, London NW1 4DF.

FOREWORD

WHEN USING A SATNAV, HAVE YOU EVER

- gone to the wrong destination?
- taken a wrong turning?
- had a near miss or crash?
- turned into a no entry street?
- wanted to plan your own route?

If you have, then this book is for you. It provides a thorough analysis of the difficulties and problems surrounding satellite road navigation, suggests solutions to common problems, and concludes with guiding principles. Satnav is viewed as a resource rather than a master, and developing your own navigational skill is shown to be surprisingly easy. The book covers dedicated handheld satnavs as well as smartphone apps and provides pointers to advanced route planning. It includes a review of a high-specification satnav with live traffic updates and concludes with an evaluation of the satnav as a concept.

The book shows how to develop knowledge, understanding, and skill when using a satnav for road navigation.

INTRODUCTION

WHO IS THE BOOK AIMED AT?

This book is aimed at drivers who own or wish to own a satnav in the United Kingdom, the United States, and beyond. The following categories of driver will find this publication of interest:

- The general motorist
- Minicab drivers
- Truckers
- Van drivers
- Motorbike riders
- Mobile engineers, managers, company representatives
- Emergency service drivers, etc.

In addition, satnav designers may also be interested.

FROM WHAT PERSPECTIVE HAS THE BOOK BEEN WRITTEN?

The book has been written by a professional driver. Other significant contributors to the debate, of which this book forms a part, are

- Consumers associations or groups
- Street atlas publishers
- Automobile associations
- Road safety groups
- Professional driver groups
- Driving skills groups
- Satnav manufacturers and others

DOES THE BOOK APPLY TO ALL SATNAVS?

The majority of techniques described can be applied to most dedicated satnavs and apps for smartphones. Some of the most popular basic-model satnavs are compared in a table in chapter 3 in relation to their route-planning features.

The book provides a guide to what can be achieved with the most versatile of the basic-model satnavs. Understanding the book will allow those who own a less versatile machine to become aware of what is possible and thereby understand the limitations of their own machine.

Most satnavs allow the destination address to be confirmed and the majority allow route familiarisation. Differences occur with route planning, but even here most allow some route adjustment.

The underlying principles of the book concern road navigation in general, and all satnav users will find this useful. A summary chart entitled 'How to Develop Skill with a Satnav' provides a snapshot of the knowledge and understanding necessary to develop skill. (See chart 1 below.) The development of skill, however, takes a considerable amount of time using a satnav for road navigation. (See 'Suggested Levels of Skill When Using a Satnav' in the appendices.)

HOW TO DEVELOP SKILL WITH A SATNAV

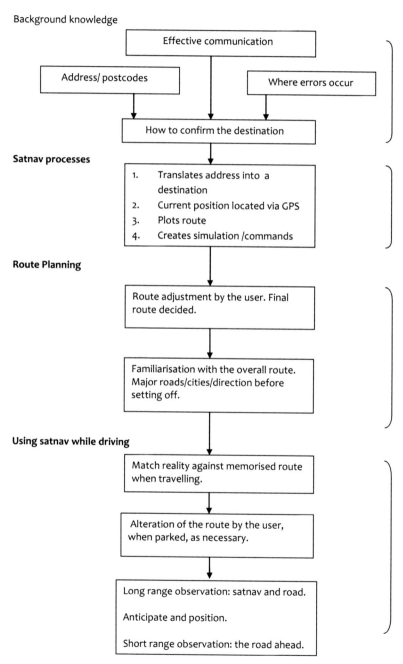

Background knowledge

Effective communication

Address/ postcodes

Where errors occur

How to confirm the destination

Satnav processes

1. Translates address into a destination
2. Current position located via GPS
3. Plots route
4. Creates simulation /commands

Route Planning

Route adjustment by the user. Final route decided.

Familiarisation with the overall route. Major roads/cities/direction before setting off.

Using satnav while driving

Match reality against memorised route when travelling.

Alteration of the route by the user, when parked, as necessary.

Long range observation: satnav and road.

Anticipate and position.

Short range observation: the road ahead.

Chart 1.

Objectives

Once you have read this book and gained practical experience putting the principles of the book into practice, you will be able to do the following with a basic-model satnav, a higher specification satnav should hold no mysteries.

1. Apply the principles of road navigation with a satnav.
2. Modify a route proposed by satnav to one which is more effective.
3. Negotiate traffic congestion more often.
4. Confirm that the location found using satnav relates to the destination address.
5. Reduce navigational errors while driving.
6. Reduce inputting errors.
7. Reduce the likelihood of taking a wrong turn or going down a no-entry street.
8. Reduce distractions, near misses, and swerves.

I have been using these techniques on a daily basis and have become a very effective road navigator as a result. Even in places unfamiliar, I can negotiate my route far better than the plodding, faltering progress I had made previously with either a street atlas or by blindly following satnav.

CHAPTER 1

Literature Search

What advice or guidance can a satnav user find in the literature to help him or her in using a satnav?

The first place to look for advice is the manufacturer. Usually a satnav is purchased with a user guide. This guide is often brief and concentrates on getting started, how to use the menu, and how to set up the satnav, but it doesn't help much beyond this. The next logical place to look is the manufacturer's website. Here manuals for each model usually provide much more detail but do little to help the reader with using a satnav in practice.

Not much seems to have been written beyond how to use the menu, and even this is not explained in the detail required to apply it for effective road navigation. How to input data to reduce error, for example, is not mentioned, and only the most cursory reference is made to planning a route. Also, no reference has been encountered regarding how to use a satnav while driving.

A wider search of US and UK literature reveals few publications that are available to help; those publications that do exist are brief and lack a driver's perspective. Nevertheless, the following most relevant publications are examined here:

- Collin's *Sat Nav Buddy.*
- *Phillip's Navigator Trucker's Britain.*
- 'Route Planner': on the Automobile Association's (AA) website.
- 'Computing guides: satnav reviews' from the Which? website.

- *Driving for Work: Vehicle Technology* (RoSPA) provides safety considerations.
- 'The Knowledge'. The way a London taxi driver learns London streets is compared and contrasted with the use of a satnav.
- Lastly, *Advanced Driving, The essential Guide*, is examined and the skills of the advanced driver are explored.

Before considering these publications in detail, a brief historical perspective is provided, followed by the results of a number of surveys. The results of these surveys, conducted by professional bodies, provide an evidence base for the problems drivers typically face when using a satnav.

HISTORY OF THE SATNAV

The satnav has been on the market for a relatively short period of time. The significant steps in the path to the present day are as follows (identified by *Philip's Navigator Trucker's Britain*):

HISTORY OF THE SATNAV

By mid 1990s	The first satnavs appeared but were luxury items.
By mid 2000	The first pocket size portable device was mass produced but was very expensive.
By 2008	35% of automobiles in the UK had a satnav 16% of automobiles in the USA had a satnav and 33% of automobiles in Japan had a satnav.

Table 1 adapted from *Philip's Navigator Trucker's Britain* 2009, p. VI.

This brief historical outline shows that the portable satnav has become popular relatively recently—within the last twenty years. This may explain why, although many of the drawbacks of using a satnav have been clearly identified, few solutions have yet been provided. Now that drivers have had a number of years of experience with portable navigation technology, perhaps it's time for satnav users to make contributions to our understanding. This book is one such attempt.

SURVEY EVIDENCE

The following survey results emerged from a literature search.

An AA/Populus Poll revealed the following for a survey conducted in 2008 of drivers' experiences:

- Almost a third of respondents said their satnav had taken them to the wrong destination.
- Forty per cent said they used satnav frequently.
- Over twenty per cent said they had been distracted by satnav while driving.
- The age range most likely to own a satnav was the 18-24 year age group, with forty-three per cent owning one (www.theaa.com).

Another survey of drivers' experiences, conducted by Direct Line and reported in *Philip's Navigator Trucker's Britain,* revealed the following:

SURVEY OF DRIVERS' EXPERIENCES BY DIRECT LINE

300,000 motorists said their satnav had caused them to crash or have a near miss.
1.5 million car drivers had veered dangerously or illegally while following satnav directions.
5 million car drivers had been sent the wrong way down a one way street.

Table 2 adapted from *Philip's Navigator Trucker's Britain* 2009, p. VI.

RESPONSE TO SURVEY RESULTS

THE MARKET

The satnav market is vast and growing, and at the leading edge are young drivers. (Note: smartphone satnav apps are also a rapidly growing market.)

WRONG DESTINATION

To prevent drivers from going to the wrong destination, a simple procedure can be used as explained in the conclusions to this book. What is interesting here is that this literature search reveals little to help drivers overcome such difficulties, except perhaps to fall back on street atlases.

DISTRACTIONS WHILE DRIVING

Distractions may be of two main types. The first is probably due to glitches, unnecessary noises, misunderstandings, misdirections, etc., while the second may be because the driver is inappropriately adjusting satnav while driving. The latter is a safety concern and must be resisted, while the former may be reduced to some extent by route familiarisation prior to the journey and focusing on the road ahead rather than satnav directions. But more about this later. In addition, satnavs are becoming increasingly distracting because more and more features are being added; this is one of the concerns raised in chapter 6.

CRASH /NEAR MISS/ VEERED DANGEROUSLY

Poor driving as a result of following satnav is probably due to inexperience and a lack of guidance on how to use a satnav effectively. See levels of skill in the appendices. Further, such problems may be mitigated by using the technique described in chapter 4. Also, an improvement to the design of a satnav might help reduce such problems. More about this in chapter 6.

Almost half of owners used it frequently

Frequent use may range from once per day to multiple trips each day. The point here is that many drivers are using a satnav often, and the more often it is used when driving, the higher the level of skill that might potentially develop. However, skill may not develop beyond a low-level plateau unless something is known about how to reach the higher levels of skill. This book provides the know-how to develop higher levels of skill even with a basic-model satnav.

Those who use satnav less frequently will also benefit from reading this book. Occasional users will become much more confident that they will reach the correct destination, and they will be aware of the principles of road navigation. This knowledge alone will put any new satnav owner in a commanding position from which to develop skill.

Wrong way down a one-way street

Going the wrong way down a one-way street is a thorny problem that probably has its roots in out-of-date maps or incorrect maps, but don't be fooled into thinking a map update will solve all the problems. It may well not. I have updated maps a number of times and found no change to the common wrong directions I experience on familiar routes. Of course, even when maps are not the issue, road layouts change, temporary road works may arise, etc. Ultimately, the driver is responsible for which direction the vehicle travels, and the priority is to keep focused on the road ahead, particularly at critical times. Route familiarisation before the journey may help, but in towns and on minor roads a driver is relying more heavily than ever on satnav. Help is provided in chapter 4, and a possible solution is suggested in chapter 6.

Which? 'Computing guides: satnav reviews'

Although prepared for the UK market, this publication provides information and advice that is valid well beyond the UK. Which? provides consumer advice on satnav purchase in its computing guides section of the its website (www.which.co.uk). Of most interest here are the sections entitled

- Satnav reviews: FAQs
- Satnav reviews: Features Explained
- Satnavs: Satnav Live Traffic

This is an excellent—probably the best available—overview of the market. The treatment doesn't go into great depth but nevertheless covers the basics very well and provides very helpful explanations of technical terms. Which? provides reviews of a very wide range of satnavs as well as advice and information to help the prospective purchaser make an appropriate choice. The wide range of satnavs includes dedicated satnavs and apps (downloaded to a smartphone).

They also mention integrated satnavs (supplied with the car) in its Features Explained section.

The Frequently Asked Questions (FAQs) section is particularly relevant to this publication, and the comments made below refer to this section.

ROUTE OPTIONS

This Which? publication is one of the few where route planning is mentioned. They say, 'Most satnavs let you select from a range of options, e.g. the quickest or the shortest route, or choose a particular waypoint or one avoiding motorways or toll roads' (Which? 2012, Satnav reviews: FAQs). Also, they mention a major road can be avoided. This backs up my assertion that most satnavs allow route planning.

LIVE TRAFFIC INFORMATION

Which? says, 'Newer traffic avoidance systems are live Internet services offered by brands such as TomTom (HD Traffic) on their mid-range and high-end satnavs. Increasingly satnav apps on mobile phones are offering live Internet traffic too' (Which? 2012, Satnav Live Traffic). They go on to say these systems are superior to TMC systems offering detailed congestion information. (TMC systems rely on information from radio stations and may not show normal commuter congestion.)

COMMENT: POSSIBLE DRAWBACKS OF LIVE TRAFFIC INFORMATION

- In the past, drivers sometimes found that congestion has passed away by the time they reached the area in question.
- Congestion information used to plot a route at the start of a journey may have become out of date halfway through the journey.

Automatic rerouting combined with HD live traffic largely solved these problems. However, despite this—or indeed because of it—herding around congestion remains an issue. In addition, from my experience, sometimes congestion on minor roads is not shown in hotspots around major road congestion.

SAFETY

On safety, amongst other things, Which? says

- Familiarise yourself with your route before setting off.
- Ensure vision isn't compromised when satnav is positioned.
- Don't blindly follow satnav directions, which are fallible and are only there to help you. (See Which? 2012, Satnav reviews: FAQs).

COMMENT ON SAFETY POINTS

Route familiarisation is a vital element of route planning, in my opinion, and has been incorporated into the principles of road navigation. (See the conclusion.) Route familiarisation is not just a safety point but also an important element in gaining mastery over satnav.

Blindly following satnav is the probable cause of many of the difficulties drivers experience. As identified in the driver surveys previously mentioned, this book is dedicated to providing drivers with the knowledge to overcome this.

'Route Planner' (AA)

A number of websites allow route planning, many more than can be mentioned here. In the UK, a few of the more notable sites are

- The TomTom website
- The Royal Automobile Club website
- The Automobile Association's website

In the United States, some route-planning sites require membership but not necessarily for a fee.

Two sites that are free and do not require membership are

- The Michelin website (www.viamichelin.com)
- The TomTom website

Perhaps one of the better websites for route planning is the Automobile Association's. These sites allow a postcode or address to be entered for both the start point and destination. Following this, the route planner generates a route which is shown as both a map and an itinerary. The map and itinerary can be printed. (See www.theaa.com.)

Before satnav arrived on the scene, many drivers relied on these route planners, particularly for longer journeys, and some drivers continue to do so. The route planner allows a road navigator to check the start and finish points and to see the route as a whole. In addition, a hard copy of the route shown on a map together with a route itinerary can be taken on the journey and used for reference when parked. The route cannot be adjusted but can be memorised and referred to during the journey, either by a passenger/navigator or when stopped.

What can a satnav user learn from a route planner?

The AA website route planner provides the usual list of roads and next-turn information, but what is significant is the inclusion of 'next road sign' directions, such as 'Head towards (a particular city or town together with the major road designation).' In fact, satnavs also have itineraries sometimes to be found in the 'exclude a road' option, but these usually only provide a list of roads. I note that TomTom Go Live 1000 provides an itinerary with the addition of good road sign directions; this is an improvement on the basic model.

What is special about the AA Route Planner

- The Route Planner shows 'next road sign' information that actually matches the real road signs to look for along the route. Note: the Route Planner does not show the name of the next minor road when this does not match any road sign in the real world.
- Road signs are displayed very realistically because they are displayed looking just like real road signs.
- They are presented as bold, easily noticed symbols.
- They are clear and effective.

The following table shows a comparison between satnav and the AA route planner.

Route Planner v. Satnav Comparison

Route Planner (AA)	Satnav
WHAT IS PROVIDED:	WHAT IS PROVIDED:
A map with a route shown on it.	A map with a route shown on it.
An itinerary.	The option to change the route.
A printed (hard copy).	An itinerary (see 'exclude a road' menu option on some satnavs).
	Real-time simulation to follow.

Route Planner (AA)	Satnav
ADVANTAGES	ADVANTAGES
An itinerary with road sign information such as the next town or city together with the road designation.	The destination and roads along the way can be examined by magnification.
A printed copy that can be examined at will.	The route can be altered.
	It may be possible to see some towns along the route by looking at the overall route map.
METHOD	METHOD
Driver becomes familiar with the route before the journey then uses memory. The memory can be refreshed as necessary during the journey.	Driver follows real time simulation but has also become familiar with the overall route, allowing memory to play a part.
DISADVANTAGES	DISADVANTAGES
The route cannot be adjusted.	Little town or city ahead information on the overall map.
Relies on driver's memory.	No town or city ahead information on the itinerary.

Table 3, Route Planner v. satnav comparison, adapted from the AA Route Planner (www.theaa.com) and the TomTom One XL user guide (www.tomtom.co.uk).

COLLIN'S SAT NAV BUDDY

Another publication that is of interest here is Collin's *Sat Nav Buddy*, and the reason it is included is because the first four pages concern the satnav. The rest of the publication comprises a list of postcodes for places of interest in Great Britain, and following this there are forty pages of maps covering Great Britain's road network. The places of interest include tourist attractions, parks, airports, and shopping centres; an index of town names and grid references are provided for the maps. The first four pages are of most interest, covering how to use a satnav. This section details choosing a satnav, using a satnav in rural areas, reducing the risk of theft, large vehicles, and how satnav works, but perhaps the most significant sections for examination are:

- Entering your destination into satnav
- Driving with your satnav
- Using the atlas with your satnav (Collin's *Sat Nav Buddy* 2009, p. 1-5)

Regarding the first of these sections, Entering your destination into satnav, I provide the following comments (See table 4).

COMMENTS ON COLLIN'S SAT NAV BUDDY:
ENTERING YOUR DESTINATION INTO SATNAV

Sat Nav Buddy	Comments
You should use the postcode to enter data because otherwise errors may occur.	This book shows that using the postcode alone presents many problems and would be therefore be unwise to use alone.
Even when the postcode is used the destination may not be pinpointed.	A good point. The postcode may only give an approximate destination. Often this is a close approximation and because it is often close to the exact location

Sat Nav Buddy	Comments
	it can mean that satnav users assume that it will always locate the correct destination. This misleading assumption can mean drivers ending up at the wrong destination from time to time without any understanding for the reason. For the reasons why postcodes do not pinpoint the exact destination see chapter 2.
Postcodes are best to use because they are not duplicated around the country. While road names may be the same in a number of towns.	It is true that road names can be the same in a number of towns however, I would disagree that using postcodes alone would be the best solution to this problem.
The publication provides eighteen pages of places of interest in Great Britain and lists postcodes for them but does not provide any addresses.	I have argued, see chapter 2, that both the postcode and the address are important elements when confirming a destination as correct. When it is not possible to have both the postcode and the address then the address should be favoured because when using a postcode alone, it is be impossible to detect any errors or omissions and impossible to confirm the destination as correct.

Table 4 adapted from Collins *Sat Nav Buddy* 2009, p. 1-5.

The following comments are provided with reference to Driving with your satnav (See table 5).

COMMENT S ON COLLIN'S *SAT NAV BUDDY*: DRIVING WITH YOUR SATNAV.

Sat Nav Buddy	Comments
Regarding safety: the display should be turned off if it is distracting.	Other alternatives are: • Satnav could be repositioned. • 3D display might be switched to 2D. • Leave on overall display but still allow voice commands.
A further safety point is to stop if a route is to be planned.	An important safety point. This is probably the most important safety point concerning driving with your satnav and although I do not refer to it in chapter 4 it is something that is mentioned throughout this book. Planning a route while travelling is probably as dangerous as using a mobile phone on the move.
Do not do what satnav says without considering the road ahead.	A good point but it needs fleshing out. Exaltations of this kind do little to actually help a driver to become a better satnav user. I have included a chapter of advice on this issue because it is a much neglected area concern. See chapter 4.
It is easier to get an overview of your route with a map because satnav is so small it is difficult to visualise the route as a whole.	It is convenient and perfectly practical to see the route as a whole on a satnav. To do this, examine the overall display then magnify or reduce the scale of the map until the

Sat Nav Buddy	**Comments**
	route as a whole can be seen. Then magnify or reduce the scale where appropriate to pick out roads, junctions etc. More town detail than on previous models is provided on satnavs such as the TomTom Go Live 1000 and this allows towns along the route to be identified quite easily.

Table 5 adapted from Collins *Sat Nav Buddy* 2009, p. 1-5.

PHILIP'S NAVIGATOR TRUCKER'S BRITAIN

The reason for the inclusion of a trucker's atlas for the UK rather than one from the US is because this publication has an introduction dealing with the satnav. For readers in the US who are interested in a trucker's atlas, one has been suggested in the Further Reading list at the end of the book. *Philip's Navigator Trucker's Britain* comprises mostly an A3-size atlas for truckers, but it has a short section of advice at the front for the motorist. The UK atlas is 1.5 miles to an inch and provides excellent detail. It starts with an introduction describing the history of the increasing popularity of the satnav over the last ten years or so. Then the advantages and disadvantages of satnavs are considered with a selection of positive and negative press reports. Of most interest here are the two pages about why you can't rely on your satnav alone. (See *Philip's Navigator Trucker's Britain* 2009 p. VI to VII.)

The following tables include a summary of the main points from these two pages and comments are provided on both (See tables 6 and 7 following).

Comments on *Philip's Navigator Trucker's Britain*

Philip's Navigator Trucker's Britain	Comments
The live traffic service may alert you too late or send you on a diversion when the original blockage has passed away.	Live internet traffic is very good compared to previous systems. Listening to local radio traffic reports also helps.
Do not follow satnav blindly or adjust it when driving.	Both good points. Also the advice on using satnav while driving helps, see chapter 4.
Advice for HGV drivers that dedicated satnavs are on the market but should not be used as a sole resource.	The Which? publication also mentions this.
Routing can be wildly indirect.	This is likely because satnav is set on fastest rather than shortest route. Learning how to adjust such routes is part of becoming a skilled operator, see chapter 3.
The increasing number of features added to satnavs may be distracting.	Particularly when features cannot be turned off by the user.
Maps may be out of date or include errors.	From my experience map updates, although essential do not solve all the problems.
Errors may occur with satnav directions.	See advice for not following satnav blindly above.

Table 6 adapted from *Philip's Navigator Trucker's Britain* 2009, p. VI to VII.

Why You Should Always Carry a Map,
according to *Philip's Navigator Trucker's Britain*

Philip's Navigator Trucker's Britain	Comments
1. You can plan your route, visualise the whole journey and ensure your heading is right.	This can also be done with a satnav by examining the overall display of the route and by magnification and reduction of the route.
2. You are less likely to get stuck on farm tracks. You tend to use major roads when using a map.	Magnification of the route allows suspect minor roads to be excluded though selection of appropriate menu options. (Identify the road then exclude it).
3. You can plan several stops with leisure driving, while a satnav is designed to get you from A to B quickly.	You can plan stops with a satnav too. Magify the route where you want to stop and discover a road name nearby by examining the screen display then enter this as a destination or highlight a road and use it as a waypoint.
4. Congestion; a satnav may give notice of a traffic hold up but will then direct you and hundreds of other satnav users onto the same diversion. Map users can go on alternative routes.	A satnav user does not need to do what a satnav suggests. The likely major alternative road to congestion can also be excluded if sufficient distance prior to the congestion allows.

Philip's Navigator Trucker's Britain	Comments
5. With an atlas you don't get a lost signal or the need to recharge or reset the satnav.	With a satnav , once you have familiarised yourself with the overall route you're in a similar position as the map reader.
6. You can have a very effective team if one person is driving and the other map reads.	This is a reasonable statement but what if you're the driver and alone?
7. Atlases are inexpensive.	Fair comment.
8. Truckers get height, width and weight information on a good quality road atlas.	True, also some satnavs are now on the market that are dedicated for HGVs

Table 7 adapted from *Philip's Navigator Trucker's Britain* 2009, p. VII.

Regarding point 3 above, where *Philip's Navigator Trucker's Britain* says you can plan stops along the way, one point in favour of using a map over a satnav is that maps show more detail and sometimes show places of interest. If this is what *Philip's Navigator Trucker's Britain* is trying to suggest, then this point might be made more clearly.

UNDERLYING ASSUMPTION

From this examination, it would seem that *Philip's Navigator Trucker's Britain* regards the use of a satnav as one where you input a destination and then simply follow satnav directions. To be fair, many drivers who are new to using a satnav or who use it rarely probably do just that.

'THE KNOWLEDGE'

Unlike New York, taxi drivers in London have to learn a considerable body of knowledge before they qualify to carry passengers. In New York, a good knowledge of the streets and a few weeks training is considered adequate, while in London many years learning the city streets are required. (See www.bls.gov/oco/ocos245.htm). Of course, the respective drivers face considerably different challenges.

London taxi drivers are required to learn London streets and places of interest to ensure they have a detailed and expert knowledge. This may take up to three years or more to learn and is referred to as 'the knowledge.'

THE KNOWLEDGE

The knowledge comprises

- A detailed understanding of the streets and places of interest within a six-mile radius of Charing Cross (considered the centre of London for the purposes of the knowledge).
- Three hundred and twenty 'runs' or routes through and reaching beyond London.
- Major points of interest within the six-mile radius (e.g., historic buildings, hotels, theatres, police stations, railway stations, leisure centres, parks, hospitals, clubs, and squares).
- It includes the main streets and side streets and the optimum routes for certain journeys. (See www.tfl.gov.uk)

Two questions arise from this outline of the knowledge: What can a satnav user learn from a London taxi driver and what can a London taxi driver learn from a satnav user?

WHAT CAN A LONDON TAXI DRIVER LEARN FROM AN EXPERT SATNAV USER?

A London taxi driver would probably learn little from an expert satnav user within the six-mile radius of the centre of London. But beyond this, a thorough knowledge of how to use a satnav might come in handy.

Logically, it would be sensible to have satnav adjusted to the shortest-route option if it is solely being used within a city centre. Although I doubt taxi drivers would need it for this purpose, except perhaps to find a destination near the end of a journey (i.e., the last quarter mile might be useful).

If a taxi driver has been requested to make a journey beyond the six-mile radius, then a satnav could prove useful, but here satnav would best be set on the fastest-route option. In fact, it is likely a taxi driver would want to keep satnav on the fastest-route option all the time but to ignore it within London or perhaps to correct the route if required since the fastest-route often means taking major roads and this may involve much greater mileage. I suggest how such a route can be corrected in chapter 3. What is likely to be useful for a taxi driver is a good, Internet-enabled satnav with HD traffic and to keep it on the overall display with the sound muted. This would provide excellent 'congestion radar', enabling the taxi driver to avoid congestion hotspots that might otherwise not be known.

WHAT CAN A SATNAV USER LEARN FROM A LONDON TAXI DRIVER?

A satnav user will, with experience, start to learn routes that are often travelled. It will then be possible to link known routes together to form longer routes or to combine a satnav route with a known route that allows traffic congestion, for example, to be avoided. This would be a halfway stage between a knowledge-based approach of the taxi driver and the procedure-based approach of the satnav user.

Taxi drivers also tend to use minor roads, and this more direct route means they have options to avoid bottlenecks and congestion. If an arterial or major road is chosen, congestion, once encountered, may not be easy to escape.

Conversely, major roads can provide a fast means of travelling to a destination if no congestion is experienced. The satnav user has to weigh up the pros and cons of each alternative route before starting a journey. Factors such as peak time or not and heading towards, through, or away from cities may be combined with other local information, perhaps from the radio or a forward journey, to inform journey planning.

RoSPA
'DRIVING FOR WORK: VEHICLE TECHNOLOGY'

Although produced in the UK, this document covers general safety points that are also useful for the US. The publication concerns safety and the use of in-vehicle technology. Primarily, it covers how to develop and implement a company health and safety policy regarding in-vehicle technology.

The technologies covered are:

- Cruise control
- Driver fatigue
- Lane departure warning
- Reversing and parking
- Adaptive front lights, and
- Tyre pressure monitoring

Driver information systems:

- Satellite navigation
- Telematics systems (e.g., PDA)

Driver speed management systems:

- Speed warnings
- Speed limiters
- Electronic braking stability systems
- Antilock braking systems
- Brake assist
- Electronic stability control

Monitoring devices:

- Vehicle monitoring (e.g., speed, seat belt, distance, and time)

Regarding the satnav, RoSPA has the following to say:

- Keep satnav out of the driver's direct view.
- If the use of a satnav causes a driver any serious problems, issues, or accidents, the driver should plan remedial action and act upon it.
- Training: drivers must become familiar with the equipment and user guide/manuals.
- Stop and park before adjusting satnav.
- Do not remove satnav from its location while driving.
- Software maps should be kept up to date.

This RoSPA publication also provides a generic health and safety policy. (See www.rospa.com.)

COMMENTS ON DRIVING FOR WORK

Most of the points made by RoSPA, relating to the satnav, are similar to other publications and have already been the subject of comments in this book. However, when RoSPA points out that drivers should become familiar with manuals, user guides, and the equipment, it must be remembered that this is only a basic safety requirement prior to using a satnav in a vehicle. Following this, but not mentioned by RoSPA, a long period of driving while using a satnav would be necessary to develop skill and confidence.

'Remedial action,' as mentioned by RoSPA, is health and safety jargon for taking steps to prevent the incident, accident, or problem from recurring. So, for example, a driver should ask, 'What can I do in future to prevent (whatever the problem is) from happening again?' Following this, the driver should make sure the solution is actually carried out and continues to be followed from then on (i.e., a new behaviour pattern should be established). RoSPA doesn't provide examples of remedial action, so it is hoped the following might provide illumination.

HYPOTHETICAL EXAMPLE OF REMEDIAL ACTION

Possible problem:

Satnav tells you to take the next turning while you're in a busy city street, but when you try to do so you find it's one way. There is little to be done at the time; you have either gone the wrong way down the street or you have managed to manoeuvre out of the situation. However, for future occasions you must make a plan to prevent this.

Possible solution:

Instead of following satnav instructions without question, you now realise that these instructions must be treated as suggestions and not as commands. At junctions, your immediate attention must be on the road ahead and road signs so that you can check out if the turn is acceptable. Hence the need to watch satnav for future junction turns well in advance of reaching them.

Remedial action to avoid illegal turns which are not recognised as such by satnav:

- Watch the road as far ahead as possible on the satnav display to be prepared well in advance for the next turn.
- On approaching a junction, turn the focus of your attention to the road signs and the road ahead rather than satnav.

The point is that knowing what is about to happen well in advance (a turn to the right, say) allows you the freedom to focus on the road ahead. This will only be the case if satnav allows you to know in sufficient time. In practice, this means looking at the top of the satnav screen to see as far into the simulated distance as is possible; this may only allow a short range and may leave barely enough time if travelling at 30 mph. The manufacturers might like to consider this for future satnav design. More about this in chapter 6.

'Advanced Driving, the essential guide'

Although Advanced Driving is a UK-based programme, the principles are valid for any country in the world. The Institute of Advanced Motorists is based in the UK and is the body responsible for the Advanced Driver test together with a framework for courses leading to this test. A book has been produced to accompany the courses, and a prospective Advanced Driver would have to develop practical experience in accordance with the principles outlined in the book before being tested.

So what is Advanced Driving? Advanced Driving concerns keen observation and judgement about road conditions together with appropriate and safe control of a vehicle to make good progress through these conditions. (See IAM, 2007, Intro.)

Key features include

- Reading the road and anticipation of hazards in good time.
- Reaction to hazards early enough and dealing with them in a planned and systematic way.
- Ensuring the vehicle is always in the right place on the road at the right time.

Advanced Driving is concerned with the skill of driving and reading the road rather than road navigation as such. In fact, little mention is made of road navigation except for a few sentences in the 'Driving in Towns' section. Here, it says, 'In a strange town consult your map or directions when it is safe to do so . . . and make a mental note of the next three or so instructions. Pull over safely when you need to check your notes again' (IAM 2007, p. 78). The book is really written for a pre-satnav driver, someone who would normally work from a street atlas or notes taken before a journey. However, the section on observation provides a very clear insight into how an advanced driver would most likely want to use a satnav, if at all.

Observation

The section on observation is particularly important because, besides dealing with all-round vision and the need for good eyesight, the Advanced Driver is continually reading the road well ahead.

'Almost all ordinary drivers only observe the road 5-20 metres in front of them so, as well as missing most upcoming dangers altogether at 60 mph they have under a second to react if a hazard appears. Advanced drivers don't have this problem; they constantly scan the area closest to them, as well as the middle distance and all the way to the horizon. One useful technique is to immediately scan the next section of road as far as you can see ahead, every time you round a bend or reach the crest of a hill. This early-warning system has massive benefits: you can often see what direction the road is going to take, identify upcoming hazards, see traffic jams early, or spot dangerous drivers or vehicles.' IAM 2007 p. 29

It is very clear from this section on observation that an Advanced Driver would likely want to use a satnav as another source of information for early warning, amongst other things.

Conclusion to Advanced Driving

An Advanced Driver would likely want a satnav to support their

- Early warning observation
  - o To allow him or her to see far ahead, farther than the road might otherwise allow.
  - o To allow him or her to know what direction the road will take beyond the next bend.
  - o To see, for example, if another turning is coming beyond the next junction.
- Lane discipline

Early warning information would be extremely useful in allowing an appropriate lane to be found or position on the road to be adopted in plenty of time.

CHAPTER REVIEW

This chapter covered the following points:

Survey evidence

- The market for satnavs is vast and growing with the leading edge being the young driver category.
- Almost a third of drivers, in the AA survey, said they went to the wrong destination.
- Many drivers reported they had either had a crash or veered dangerously because of the satnav (AA and Direct Line).
- A significant number of drivers said they had been distracted while using a satnav (Direct Line).

Route planner v. satnav

- This comes in the form of a printed map together with an itinerary.
- The itinerary has 'next road sign' direction and information, such as, 'You are heading towards (a city or town together with major road designations like 'To Brighton, M23').
- You can memorise the route before the trip and refresh your memory at convenient stops.

Disadvantages of the route planner

- You can't refresh your memory while driving.
- You can't adjust the route.

Advantages of satnav

- You can adjust the route before the journey, also if you stop along the way.
- You can become familiar with the route before the journey.
- You can see what to do next as you travel.
- You can confirm the destination as correct.

Collin's *Sat Nav Buddy*

- Provides the postcodes for a long list of places of interest.
- Argues the postcode should be used to enter data with no road or town name necessary.
- Suggests the distance and direction are useful to check the destination is correct.
- Suggests it may be better to switch off the display if it is distracting.
- Says you should stop if you want to adjust satnav.
- Says you should not do what satnav says without considering the road ahead.

Why maps are useful (*Sat Nav Buddy*)

- To get an overview of the route.
- You cannot visualise the route with a satnav because the screen is so small.
- Maps allow a wider understanding of the route and surrounding areas.
- A map allows you to find suitable places to break a journey.

Philip's Navigator Trucker's Britain

- Don't slavishly follow satnav directions.
- Don't adjust satnav while driving.
- Many drivers reported they had been to the wrong destination.
- Many drivers reported errors, such as directing you the wrong way en route.
- More and more information is being crammed into satnav (too much).
- Maps may be out of date.
- Traffic congestion information, via live systems, may be either too late or last too long.
- You may be directed down unsuitable roads.
- Bugs or glitches may occur en route, misdirecting you.
- You may be sent on inappropriate roads for your type of vehicle.

Why maps are useful (*Philip's Navigator Trucker's Britain*)

- You can visualise the whole journey and plan.
- You are less likely to be stuck on farm roads.
- You can plan stops along the way.
- You can avoid the herd by planning with a map.
- You don't get glitches or lost signals.
- Truckers can get height, width, and weight information on appropriate atlases.

'The Knowledge', taxi driver v. satnav user

Taxi driver

- Knowledge focused.
- London focused.
- Can link short runs through London to form longer routes.
- Relatively short distances for each route or run.

Satnav user

- May travel long distances throughout the country or perhaps beyond.
- Procedure focused.
- Relies on memorised route and satnav prompts during a journey.
- The more experienced may be guided by the six principles of road navigation with a satnav.
- Likely to travel longer distances than a taxi driver.

Which? Consumer advice: satnav reviews

- Different route options are possible with most satnavs.
- Live internet traffic updates cover both major roads and minor roads with top-end model satnavs; often a basic-level model satnav does not provide this information.

Safety considerations, Which?

- Familiarise yourself with the route before the journey.
- Don't blindly follow satnav.
- Keep satnav out of the line of vision.

RoSPA safety points

- Keep satnav out of the driver's direct view.
- If the use of satnav causes any serious issues, problems or accidents, plan remedial action and act on it.
- Training drivers must become familiar with the equipment, user guide, and manuals.
- Stop and park before adjusting satnav.
- Do not remove satnav from its location while driving.
- Software maps must be kept up to date.
- A generic health and safety policy is provided.

Advanced driving

The following conclusions are drawn from this section:

- Satnav could be used to support an early-warning system.
- An early-warning system will help with lane discipline.

CHAPTER 2

Difficulties Associated with
Inputting an Address or Postcode

UNDERSTANDING POSTCODES IN THE UK

Unlike the US where the five digit zip code presents little difficulties, some satnav users in the UK experience problems understanding where within the postcode numbers are usually placed and where letters are positioned. This confusion can often lead to errors when certain letters or numbers are input (e.g., a zero or a letter O, or a number 1 or a letter I). In this section, the postcode is analysed. A typical postcode is shown as follows:

Analysis of a postcode

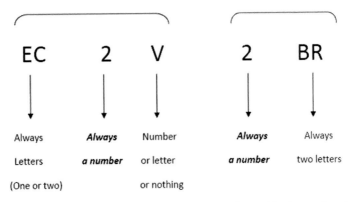

According to h2g2 on the Notpanicking website, postcodes were designed by the postal service to allow operatives to find delivery areas. They are usually split into two parts the outward and the inward. So considering the same postcode example show above, they breakdown the postcode as follows:

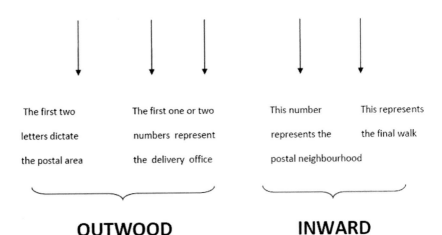

Table 8 adapted from http://h2g2.com/dna/h2g2/alabaster/A12338615.com. (Note: the h2g2 website is owned by Not Panicking Ltd.)

According to h2g2, postcodes help you to find the right local area but might locate a wrong street nearby or the wrong place on a street. Elsewhere on the same website, the author says, 'If you want to find where you are going or which county a town is in, don't rely on a postcode, use a map.' (See http://h2g2.com/dna/h2g2/alabaster/A12338615.com.)

The author here means look up the *address* in a map rather than use the postcode. This confusion with postcodes leads me to examine what would constitute the minimum information necessary to find an address.

Minimum information needed to find an address:

Option A	Option B
building number	building number
road name	road name
postcode	town and county (with country)

However, although the minimum of information will allow an address to be located, such information would have to be accurate. And in practice, the more information known about the address, the better.

A fully detailed address might include the following: addressee building thoroughfare road name estate town post town/city county and postcode

COMMENT

It would be foolish to set off on a journey

- Without a road or street name
- With only a postcode
- With, generally speaking, no number for the building on the street
- (Note: some buildings do not have numbers.)

INTERNAL CROSS-CHECKS THAT CAN BE MADE WITH AN ADDRESS IN THE UK

A number of cross-checks can be made with an address:

- The postcode can be checked against the town (e.g., PO for the Portsmouth area).

- The postcode can be checked against the road name. This can be done using satnav. Enter the postcode, and see if see if the destination is the correct road. (To do this, magnify the destination). Note: the road may be nearby rather than exactly located.
- Has sufficient information been provide to enable the address to be found?

(See minimum information needed for an address above.)

THE PROBLEM OF PINPOINTING A DESTINATION USING A POSTCODE

In summary, postcodes were never designed to pinpoint an address:

- They are inherently imprecise and provide only a close approximation to the location.
- A further problem is that the postcode provided to you may be wholly or partly inaccurate.
- Lastly, errors may occur when entering the postcode into satnav. A postcode template for the UK is shown in the book's conclusion, which may help to reduce confusion when inputting digits.

What is needed therefore is a procedure or procedures to prevent errors being translated into an incorrect destination.

Of course, any proposed procedure cannot correct an address that is fundamentally wrong and therefore the most that can be achieved is to accurately reach the address provided rather than to read the mind of the person providing it.

A NOTE ON ZIP CODES FOR THE US

In the US, the typical five-digit zip code only serves to find the general location and local city; the remainder of the address can then be entered: the town, road, and number on the road. Input errors can still occur. (See 'Inputting an Address for the USA' in the conclusion). Of course, errors can occur with the zip code itself. It may be completely wrong or include errors. Or errors may be made while inputting the digits. Always magnify the destination to confirm the road name. Input the full address rather than using the zip code if you have any doubt about the destination.

CONCLUSIONS TO 'UNDERSTANDING POSTCODES IN THE UK'

Postcodes

- Were never designed to pinpoint an address
- Should be cross-checked to correct for any inaccuracy
- May be provided to you with errors
- May involve confusion and error when input into satnav

COMMUNICATION

Often people assume that giving a command or instruction will necessarily result in implementation; however, this is by no means certain. Effective communication is a complex process, and this is as true for human-to-human interaction as it is when via a machine.

What is communication? 'Although not simple to define communication may be characterised as the transmission and reception of a message or idea from one party to another in such a fashion that it is mutually understandable' (Eyre 1982, p. 132).

It is my contention that errors of communication can be greatly reduced by understanding this book and putting that understanding into practice. An understanding of effective communication is central to developing skill with a satnav.

EFFECTIVE COMMUNICATION

In order to understand the nature of communication as it relates to the use of a satnav, communication theory is first examined, and then this is applied to the use of a satnav. For a general discussion of what makes effective communication, see chapter 14 of E. C. Eyre's *Mastering Basic Management*.

HAS THE MESSAGE BEEN RECEIVED AND UNDERSTOOD?

Just because a message has been sent, this does not mean it will have been received. Nor does it mean it will have been understood. The simplest way to find out if the message has been understood is to ask the person who received the message what the message means.

Note: Electronic messages via emails or PDAs often include a feedback system to allow the sender to know if the message has been received and if the message has been actioned. But these do not necessarily mean the message was understood. In other words, it can still be misinterpreted.

WHO IS ULTIMATELY RESPONSIBLE FOR A MESSAGE?

When you think about it, no other person can be held responsible for a message being received and understood than the person who sent it. Yet sometimes the receiver is blamed for the failure to carry out instructions which, while clearly articulated, are nevertheless open to interpretation. The sender considers the receiver to be at fault because the instruction was clearly outlined, but the real blame lies with the sender for not gaining feedback. The sender cannot be said to have communicated unless he or she has obtained satisfactory feedback. Otherwise, the sender can only be said to have issued an instruction.

FAMILIARITY OF SENDER AND RECEIVER

Difficulties arise when the sender and receiver of a message are not familiar with each other, and sometimes difficulties remain, due to psychology, attitudes, and differing levels of education. Any of these difficulties may mean that the receiver does not pay close enough attention to the content of a message. However, with experience, a more effective relationship should develop.

VERIFICATION OR FEEDBACK

As previously mentioned, making sure a message has been received and has been understood is critical to effective communication. The response may be in a verbal or written form and should satisfy the sender, who has ultimate responsibility for the message.

ACCURACY AND PRECISION

It may seem obvious that a message should be accurate and precise, but there are many reasons why this will not always be so. Examples are when a message has been created in haste or when the person creating the message has little understanding of the consequences of an inaccurate message and therefore perhaps does not take sufficient care with the details. (See Eyre 1982, chapter 14.)

CONCLUSIONS TO 'COMMUNICATION'

In conclusion, the following four main points are significant:

- The sender of a message is responsible to ensure it has been received and is understood.
- Familiarity between the sender and receiver is important (together with any other links in the chain of communication).
- Verification or feedback is essential.
- Accuracy and precision are essential.

Note: In addition to these points, a message may be distorted at any stage in its transmission. It follows, therefore, that the more links in the chain of transmission, the more possibilities of errors.

EFFECTIVE COMMUNICATION VIA A SATNAV

If the definition of communication put forward by Eyre is accepted, then two sentient beings are a prerequisite for the transmission of a message: one to send and one to receive the message. This will usually be the case, but when using a satnav it is a little different. Of course, this begs the question, can a satnav understand? To which the answer must be, 'No.' However, if the satnav *user* is considered as both the receiver of the message as well as the sender, then this apparent problem may be overcome. Satnav is, in fact, a translation device (amongst other things) and translates an address into a destination on a map. It is up to the user to both send the original message (the address) and also to interpret or comprehend the destination, found by satnav, as the receiver of the message.

As an aside, satnav appears to have four main functions:

THE FOUR MAIN FUNCTIONS OF A SATNAV

1. Translates the address into a destination
2. Locates the current position via the global positioning system (GPS)
3. Calculates and plots a route from the current position to the destination via roads in-between
4. Produces a step-by-step virtual reality simulation of the route together with voice commands, which is usually *driven* by the GPS location

It is the translation function that is of concern when the address or postcode is input.

LINKS IN THE CHAIN OF COMMUNICATION WHEN CONFIRMING A DESTINATION

Before considering communication directly via a satnav, it is important to realise that an address may have passed through a number of hands before it reaches the satnav user.

Chart 2.

The chain of communication from obtaining an address or destination through to inputting it into satnav will involve at least three distinct stages and often more; see chart 2 above. With the first two links in the chain, the general communication theory applies. With the second two links in the chain, communication theory as applied to a satnav is relevant; see below.

Application of Communication Theory to the Use of a Satnav

The sender is responsible to ensure that the message has been understood

In the case of a satnav, you are responsible to ensure satnav locates the correct destination. However, if you find any fault with the address, this should be raised with the provider before the start of the journey. Verifying that the address provided matches the location found by satnav is the key process in communicating through a satnav; this fulfils the essential feedback necessary for effective communication. Whether the address translated by satnav is correct can only be answered by you, not satnav.

FAMILIARITY

The more often the satnav is used, the more the user becomes familiar with it and the greater the degree of skill that should ensue. Such skill develops, provided that satnav is used in the context of navigating a vehicle rather than using satnav without travelling anywhere. Experience and understanding of how to input addresses, verify destinations, and follow routes are all aspects of this skill.

VERIFICATION OR FEEDBACK

Once magnified, the roads at the destination on a satnav overall route display allow for the destination to be cross-checked against the address. The following questions can be asked:

- Is the road correct?
- Is the number on the road correct? (Note: not all satnavs show road numbers.)
- Is the general location correct?
- Are the distance and direction from the start point about right?

Once these questions have been answered satisfactorily, verification is complete.

Accuracy and Precision

Inputting the address or postcode accurately is the first consideration of the satnav user, and knowing where within the postcode numbers and letters are usually positioned is an aspect of this. Ultimately, accuracy and precision can be measured when the address is verified or cross-checked. A satnav user cannot determine if an address provided is accurate or not. However, if any internal inconsistencies are found, these can be reported back to the provider. In addition, if an address cannot be found using satnav or by using a good-quality map, then this should also be reported back. It is risky driving to a destination that has not been verified.

Conclusions to 'Communication with Regard to a Satnav'

The satnav user

- Is responsible for ensuring the address provided is correctly located by satnav
- Should ensure accuracy and precision when an address or postcode is input
- Should verify whether the address has been correctly located by cross-checking it
- Should develop familiarity or skill through using a satnav on successive journeys
- Can only communicate through satnav, not with it

Where Errors Occur

This section concerns the errors associated with inputting an address (including the postcode). Chart 3 shows the main stages of using a satnav as input, process, and output. Consideration here is with the first stage and a prior pre-input stage (not shown).

Understanding Where Errors Occur

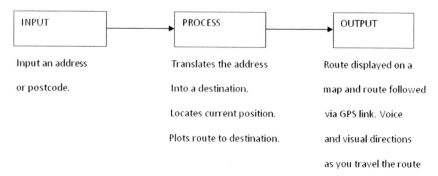

INPUT	PROCESS	OUTPUT
Input an address or postcode.	Translates the address Into a destination. Locates current position. Plots route to destination.	Route displayed on a map and route followed via GPS link. Voice and visual directions as you travel the route

Chart 3.

At the pre-input stage

This is the stage where most problems occur, and you have no control over it. The originator of the address may not be the person providing you with the address. In fact, the address may have passed through a number of hands before it is finally input into a satnav. Any element of an address maybe wrong, misspelled, or omitted. Just to give one pertinent example, if an address has been taken over the telephone, the number 2-6 may be easily misunderstood to mean 226. Many other similar examples could be cited. Suffice to say, the longer the chain of links in the transmission of the address to the satnav user, the more likely that errors may be incorporated.

You may be able to detect some errors before entering an address, such as the example previously given regarding mismatch between the postcode and the county (UK); however, which one is right might be difficult to confirm. Inputting each one and then checking the road found by satnav is likely to help.

At the input stage

• You may find the road found by satnav does not match the road in the address when the postcode is input.

- You might find that satnav does not recognise the road in the address (i.e., it does not appear on the satnav map).
- There may be a user error inputting the address or postcode.
- The satnav map may be out of date or may incorporate errors.
- The postcode may not be recognised. As you input the postcode, satnav will display the closest match it holds in reply. If these do not match, satnav will not find the correct location.

CONCLUSIONS TO 'WHERE ERRORS OCCUR'

PRE-INPUT STAGE

- Any element of the address (including the postcode) may be wrong or omitted.
- Errors may arise from any stage when an address has passed through a number of hands.
- The provided address may incorporate errors, but these may be not easy to detect.
- The address may have errors that are easily detected.

INPUT STAGE

- The road found by satnav does not match the road in the address when the postcode is input.
- User error may occur when digits are input.

HOW TO VERIFY A DESTINATION AS CORRECT

It is important to be aware of potential problems when an address/ postcode is input. However, correcting errors does not require the user to go through a list. Instead, all that is necessary is to confirm that the destination is correct. Of course, errors may still occur, but these will then be due to the original address/postcode rather than the user or satnav. In order to verify a destination as correct, I show three flow charts (charts 6, 7, and 8) below.

Why using the postcode on its own is insufficient to find a destination (for the UK)

When a postcode is used to input into satnav, the only sure way to know if satnav has found the correct destination is to magnify the destination and check what is shown. In other words, the results of satnav's translation need to be examined and interpreted by someone who knows what a correct translation would look like. However, if you are using the postcode alone, then what is displayed by magnification cannot be checked because there is nothing to check it against. What is needed therefore is an address as well as the postcode. This allows the postcode-found destination to be confirmed by cross-checking it against the road in the address. This is a sure way to confirm the destination as correct and provides the verification or feedback necessary for effective communication.

Quick method of verification even when using the address alone

Magnify the destination and check the road is correct. (Some satnavs also allow the number on the road to be seen, or at least the numbers before and after the location). The general area and direction can also be examined and a judgement made about the approximate distance.

Other checks that can be made

When a postcode is input, does satnav replicate this as entered? When an address is input, is the town (and county) followed by the road name replicated as entered?

Conclusions to 'Verification of a Destination'

- If a postcode is input, check it is replicated as input then magnify the destination and check the road name is correct. Lastly, examine the area and general route.
- When an address is input, check the town and road names replicated as entered? Then magnify the destination and, as before, check the area and general route.

HOW TO VERIFY A DESTINATION AS CORRECT WHEN A POSTCODE IS INPUT FOR THE UK

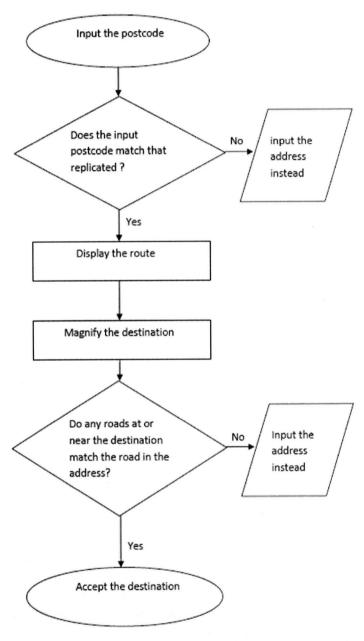

Chart 4.

How to Verify a Destination as Correct When an Address Is Used (UK and USA)

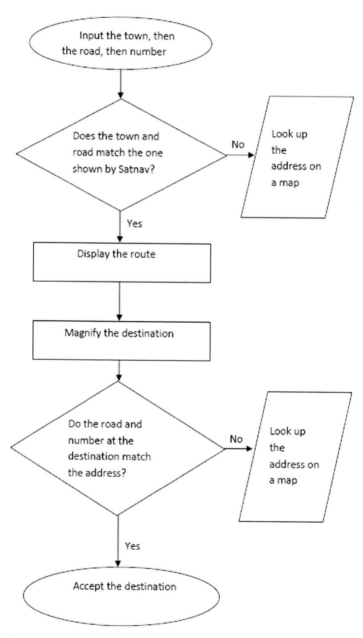

Chart 5.

How to Verify a Destination as Correct When an Atlas Is Used (UK and USA)

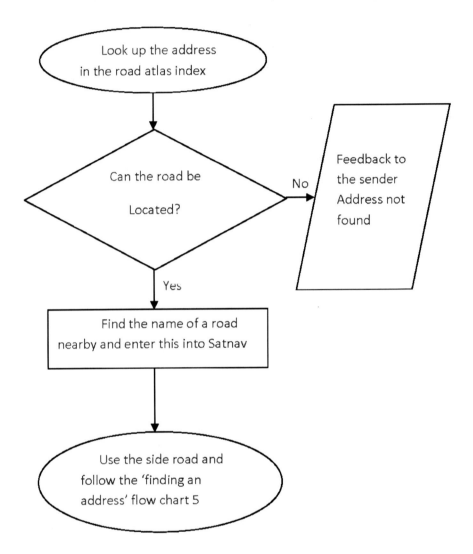

An atlas is likely to be used for two main reasons:

- Satnav does not recognise the address or postcode or
- To confirm a destination as correct (verification)

Chart 6.

Chapter Conclusion

The whole process of inputting a postcode or address into a satnav is fraught with difficulties and potential confusion. It is little wonder that drivers have problems using a satnav. What is needed, therefore, is a simple procedure (or procedures) that cuts thought the fog of misunderstanding and possible errors. The flow charts 4, 5, and 6 in the 'Verification of a Destination' section provide straightforward and clear procedures. Further practical advice is provided in the conclusion to the book.

Chapter Review

This chapter covered the following points:

Postcodes

- May not pinpoint an address.
- Must be cross-checked.
- May be partly or wholly wrong.
- May cause confusion and error when digits are input.

Communication

- You are responsible for pinpointing the destination and not the satnav.
- Accuracy and precision are essential when digits are input.
- Verification that satnav has accurately found the destination is essential.
- You must be familiar with using it for driving.
- You can only communicate through satnav, not with it.

Where errors occur

- Any element of the address (including postcode) may be wrong or omitted.
- Errors may arise from any stage in the transmission of the address to the satnav user.
- The address may incorporate an easily detected error.

- The address may be incorrect, but this cannot be detected.
- The road name and town may not match the postcode.
- Errors may occur when digits are input.

How to verify a destination as correct (confirmation)

- Check the postcode is replicated as input, if using the postcode.
- Check the town and city are replicated as input, if using the address.

Even when the input is replicated exactly:

- Magnify the destination;
  Check the road is correct.
  Check the town is correct.
  Check the number on the road, if your satnav allows this.
- Check that the general direction and distance are about right.

CHAPTER 3

Route Planning:
How to Be More Effective Than Satnav

Most satnav users are able to input an address or postcode, but how can the route generated be changed to one of your own desire? How can you gain control of the route displayed so that you develop your own navigation skills? To be in control, you need 'handles' or 'levers' to pull so you can manipulate the route.

This chapter explains how to gain control and suggests various techniques to improve on Satnav-generated routes. This advice applies to basic-model satnavs but can equally be useful when using a satnav with live traffic updates.

Firstly, what features of the *menu* allow you to gain control? The answer depends on the model of satnav used. Some allow only limited interaction while the best of the basic-model satnavs allow a number of 'levers' that can be used (and some of them in combination). Table 9, below, shows a comparison of three basic-model satnavs together with an app for a smartphone. You can see from the comparison table that both TomTom and Garmin provide similar features for route manipulation.

All the satnav models allow magnification and reduction, a vital feature used to confirm a destination as correct and for route familiarisation.

Both TomTom and Garmin allow for a road to be excluded. This is quite a useful option since it allows a known congested road to be excluded. However, by using an alternative road, a similar result can be achieved.

With less sophisticated models, the main method of route alteration is by using the 'generate an alternative route' option. Here satnav generates the alternative rather than the user, but this can be done repeatedly until a desired route is found so that the user has the final decision.

All the satnavs in the table can be used to apply the key aspects of the advice in this book.

Comparison of basic-model satnavs, showing route-planning features

INTERACTIVE FEATURE	TomTom	Garmin	Navman	Google maps app for a Smartphone
Input of address or postcode	Yes	Yes	Yes	Yes
Use a different road	Yes	Via a Waypoint	Touch screen allows road selection and a further menu allows you to add to trip	No
Magnification and reduction	Yes	Yes	Yes	Yes
Exclude a road	Yes	Yes, via Avoidances	No	No
Recalculate the original route	Yes	Yes, via Recent destination	Yes, via Recent destination	
Overall display showing towns	Yes	Yes	No	Yes
Satnav generates an alternative route	Yes	Yes	No	Yes

Comparison of basic-model satnavs, showing route-planning features

Visible road names on magnification	Yes	Yes	Yes	Yes
Automatic rerouting	Yes	Yes	Yes	Yes
	© 2009TomTom International BV	Copyright © 1996-2012 Garmin Ltd	© 2011 MITAC	© 2011 Google
Note1: Comparison based on basic models of three popular satnavs and one app for a smartphone. Please note the comparison here is with the Google maps app for a smartphone (with navigation), not to be confused with Google maps. Note2: Some early Garmin models do not allow route planning.				

Table 9 is based on user guides and manuals from the following websites:

- www.google.com/mobile/navigation/
- www.tomtom.com
- www.navman.com
- www.garmin.com

Using the Menu

Obviously, knowing how to use the menu is fundamental to route planning. Fortunately, this familiarisation can be done in the comfort of your own home rather than in your vehicle.

Menu options are vast, and rather than dealing with the entire menu, I confine my comments here to route-planning and associated activities.

So what has to be mastered?

- The menu terminology
- How to select the menu options
- How to use the touch screen to select a road
- How to use the magnification and reduction feature

The concepts involved in route planning are the same with different makes and models of satnav, but terminology and procedures differ. It is essential to become familiar with the menu options and the touch screen. Regarding the TomTom menu, some further advice can be found on the TomTom website or in the manuals for most models. However, a trial-and-error approach to menu navigation will also yield the required result.

How to use the magnification and reduction feature

Magnification and reduction controls differ with different satnav makes and models; often a positive and negative symbol appears in the top left hand and bottom corners of the screen (with some makes these are to the right) and some have a scroll bar to one side of the screen. In addition, most makes allow the whole map to move from side to side by using any part of the screen to touch and drag.

TomTom menu options for route manipulation

The following flow chart shows an example of the menu options of a popular make of satnav.

Some of the TomTom menu options that allow you to take control

Stage1. Input the address and allow satnav to generate a route.

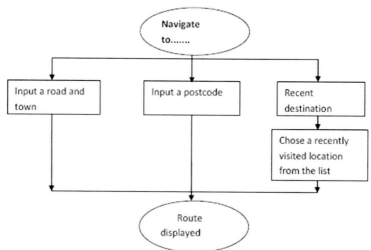

Stage2. The following options allow route manipulation.

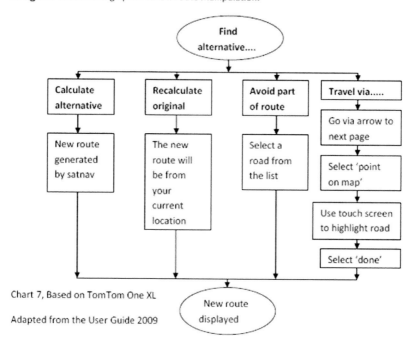

Chart 7, Based on TomTom One XL

Adapted from the User Guide 2009

ROUTE PLANNING

With the most popular makes of satnav, there are three main ways to modify a route:

- Use an alternative road.
- Exclude a road.
- Generate an alternative route.

Note: *any of these methods may be used in combination* with many makes of satnav.

Once an address or postcode has been entered and confirmed as correct, the overall map of the route can be examined.

This may become the final route once it has been evaluated by the user.

Before considering possible alternative roads to use, first check the setting of your satnav. Two settings are significant here: the shortest and fastest route options. The following table allows a comparison.

Comparison of fastest and shortest route options

Fastest Route	Shortest Route
Advantages	**Advantages**
Uses major roads	The most direct route, often using minor roads
Quickest route, theoretically	Less fuel used
Effortless driving, little gear changing	Maybe better for city centres

Fastest Route	Shortest Route
Disadvantages	**Disadvantages**
Covers long distances, often many miles out of the way	May take a much longer time when actually travelling because of local congestion. Therefore the estimated time of arrival (ETA) will be unrealistic
Alternative routes that may be more direct may be rejected because they take minutes more	
Routes that take an initial short distance in the opposite direction may be discounted	

Table 10 is based on personal experience.

CONCLUSIONS TO THE COMPARISON OF FASTEST AND SHORTEST ROUTE OPTIONS

Most satnav users adopt the 'fastest route' option. However, this option has major drawbacks. (See comparison table 10.) The fastest route can mean travelling many miles more than needed. It seems the 'fastest route' option is more suitable for longer journeys and the 'shortest route' option is for shorter trips, particularly city centres.

My own preference is to leave satnav on the 'fastest route' option but to use the techniques described in this book to correct for excesses.

Firstly, it is important to understand how satnav plans routes so that the user can go beyond the 'mindset' of satnav.

How satnav plans routes

If satnav could plan a direct route from A to B, then it would, as shown in figure 1.

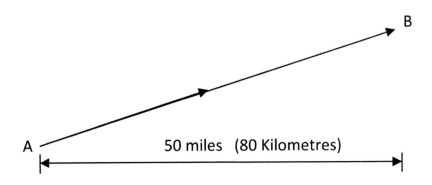

Figure 1.

Satnav cannot plan a direct route because it has to follow the roads that fill the gap between A and B. So a satnav route may look more like that shown in figure 2 or 3, because either/both of these routes fit the roads available.

A 'best-fit,' satnav-generated route

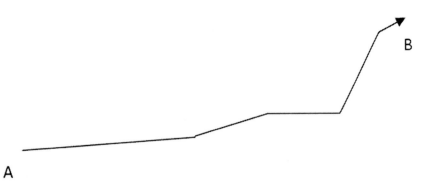

Figure 2.

An alternative 'best-fit,' satnav route

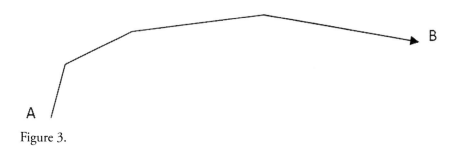

Figure 3.

The 'best route'

What satnav does not do is to provide the only route or even the 'best route' between two points. In fact, there is no 'best route,' only one of many possibilities. Some may be shorter in distance but marginally longer in time. Or they may be longer in distance, but because they involve major roads, they may take less time in practice. You can see this for yourself by selecting 'generate alternative' from the menu then repeat this action a number of times. You can also compare the ETAs. It should be noted that routes involving minor roads often take much longer than predicted because of traffic lights, roundabouts, local congestion, road works, etc.

How to develop your own navigational skills

The first rule to follow is never accept the route proposed by satnav. You then become increasingly involved in your own navigation. Maybe the satnav route will be accepted eventually, but only after considering and planning a number of alternatives.

ROUTES NOT LIKELY TO BE PLANNED BY SATNAV

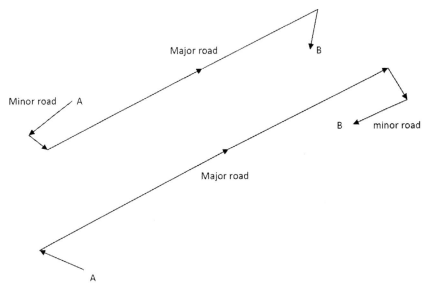

Figure 4.

Considering the previous example, showing how satnav plans routes, as shown in figure 2 and figure 3. Figure 4 shows how a user might adapt either of these routes to better effect.

Although somewhat exaggerated, either of the two examples shown as figure 4 show how user thinking can go beyond the 'mindset' of satnav. These routes take advantage of the major roads nearby rather than the minor roads of the original satnav route shown in figures 2 and 3. Satnav would not initially plan either of these routes because the major roads are not on a direct path to the destination. Major road affords a higher speed and few, if any, stops. This is a big advantage over using minor roads, providing traffic conditions allow.

1. Using an Alternative Road

How can you know a better alternative road to the main road in the satnav proposed route?

- **Use a parallel major road as an alternative**

A possible technique to adopt in order to achieve an improved route is the use of an alternative, parallel, major road. Major roads are often better to use than minor roads even at peak times. To plan this, first magnify and examine the route satnav has generated, then look each side of this route for an alternative, major, parallel road. The alternative does not need to be exactly parallel and can be easily picked out because it will be a thicker and more defined road. Select one as an alternative road, and allow satnav to complete the details of the new route.

This alternative major road option works best in cities but can be used more widely; the technique is illustrated in figure 5.

The 'alternative major road' technique.

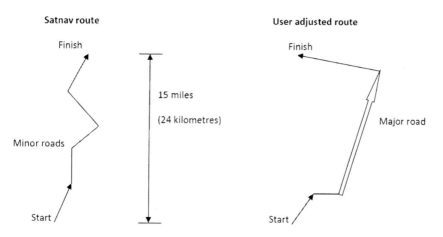

Figure 5.

Using a parallel major road would be suitable for most situations and most drivers. But taxis, prefer not to be stuck on a major road where congestion is possible, as mentioned previously, because they may become trapped. Such drivers are likely to prefer the minor the roads of the original route.

BACKFLIP

The backflip allows the road navigator access to a major road that would otherwise not be on a direct path to the destination. Consider figures 6 and 7.

SATNAV ROUTE BEFORE THE BACKFLIP HAS BEEN PLANNED

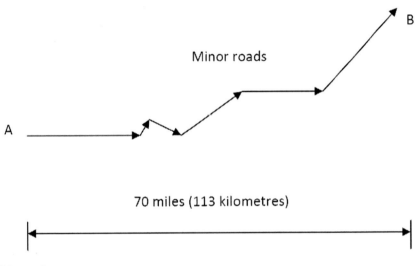

Figure 6.

User-adjusted route: the backflip

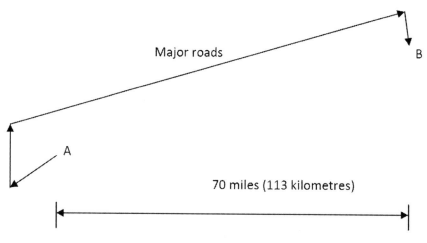

Figure 7.

Although the user-adjusted route is longer in distance, it takes advantage of a nearby major road, which allows high, uninterrupted speeds. Over this distance, the major road is worth taking. Note: this may not be the case at peak times.

How to plan the backflip

Try selecting the major road as an alternative road. If satnav does not allow this, then magnify the major road at the point you wish to join it and look for a junction. If you find a junction within, say, five miles of your start point, then simply drive in that direction until satnav redirects you along the major road. Alternatively, find the name of a road near the major road junction by magnification and input this as your next destination. Once you reach this road, stop. Then from recent destinations, select your original destination and satnav will now use the major road. Another interesting technique that goes beyond the mindset of satnav is what I have termed the 'slingshot.'

The Slingshot

The slingshot involves continuing on a major road to gain a time advantage over the original satnav route. (See figures 8 and 9.)

Satnav route before planning the slingshot

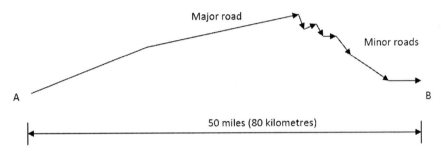

Figure 8.

Satnav will plan a route that is as direct as possible from A to B. If this route can be modified by the user to follow more of the major road before heading to the final destination, then a boost or slingshot effect will have been achieved. This technique uses fewer minor roads and therefore wastes less time.

How to plan the slingshot

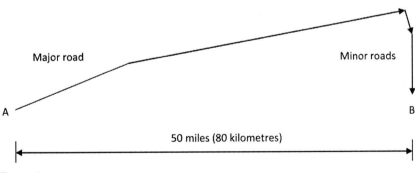

Figure 9.

Figure 9 shows much more of the major road used before turning off to head for the destination. To do this, use the 'alternative road' menu option and select more of the same major road. Following this, satnav will automatically complete your route to your destination.

REVERSE SLINGSHOT

When you're at a new location and then plan a further trip, satnav can suffer from the 'mindset' issue referred to previously. Here, satnav plans a route to your next destination that may take many miles of minor roads before joining a major road. This can mean a huge amount of unnecessary time being wasted, especially at peak times, and it is also difficult to notice when first looking at the route. The problem is shown in figure 10.

SATNAV ROUTE BEFORE PLANNING THE REVERSE SLINGSHOT

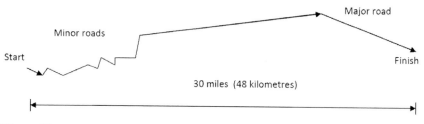

Figure 10.

User adjusted route: reverse slingshot

Figure 11.

To improve on the Satnav route, first magnify the initial stage, then plan to join the major road as soon as possible.

2. EXCLUDE A ROAD

Why would you need to exclude a road? There may be many reasons why you might like to do this. Some that readily come to mind are as follows:

- Peak-time congestion is known to be bad on a particular road.
- A road is nearly always congested throughout the day.
- You discover a road is congested before setting off, perhaps via the radio.

It is a good idea to develop a list of roads that should be avoided. These will become known to you with experience.

Within a city, you might have a list of four or more roads you always avoid. These are likely to be important long roads. You might also develop a list of alternative roads that are preferred to the roads to be avoided.

GATHERING INFORMATION ON CONGESTION

How do you gather information on congestion? This knowledge develops over time, but some sources are detailed as follows:

- The flow of traffic in and out of cities during morning and evening peak times is an important consideration.
- Listening to traffic information on the radio is a second source of information.
- Traffic conditions noted on a forward journey can be useful on a return trip.
- Major roads often have electronic sign congestion information.
- If you are prepared to pay a tariff, you might use a satnav with live traffic updates, although this might be more relevant to major roads.
- In the UK, the following publication and websites are useful to identify known congestion hotspots:
  - *The Complete Driver's Atlas of Britain and Ireland,* 2004
  - The TomTom Route Planner (www.tomtom.com)
  - The highways agency website (www.highways.gov.uk)

3. Generate an Alternative Route

Most satnavs appear to have the facility to generate an alternative route; it is the most basic form of the route manipulation and the quickest and easiest way to obtain an alternative route. You have no control over the alternative route generated, but by repeating the alternative route a number of times, a range of alternatives can be produced and you can decide on the most appropriate. Decide which route you prefer—the first, second, third, or fourth—then go through 'recent destination option' and select the same destination (or input the address again and generate an alternative). This reproduces the original route and you then go through each alternative once more until the preferred route is replicated again.

Drawbacks

- The whole route will be replaced with an alternative; this may be good with a relatively short route but may be inappropriate for a long-distance route.
- No fine-tuning or adjustments of the route are possible. However, if you have a satnav that allows the other route manipulation techniques, then, as mentioned before, this form of route manipulation can be used with any of the others, provided your satnav is so enabled.

4. Correction of an Excessively Long Satnav Route

One other phenomenon that occurs to the satnav user is the generation of an excessively long route by satnav for no apparent reason. Such a route will be generated because satnav has been set or programmed to find the 'fastest' route, and it does this by using major roads with high average speeds. An example of an excessively long route is shown in figure 12. The route produced by satnav may be quicker by only a few minutes than an alternative route, such as that shown as the correction to the route also in figure 12. But the excessively long route is about a third longer!

CORRECTING AN EXCESSIVELY LONG SATNAV ROUTE

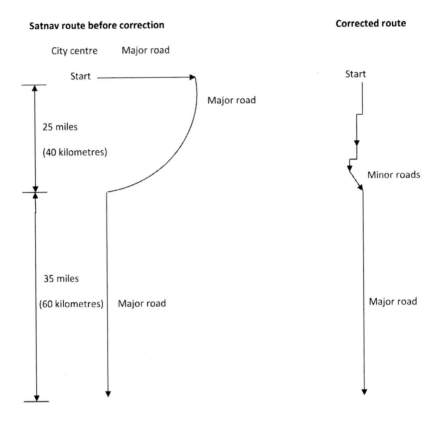

Figure 12.

CLARIFICATION OF THE PROBLEM

The estimated time of arrival (ETA) is based on the average speed of the roads involved. However, the average speed has been calculated on the equivalent of a good day when little, if any, traffic is about (e.g., a Sunday morning when the roads are clear). Such ETAs are only realistic for clear major roads. When minor roads are used, even with light traffic, ETAs become optimistic; with heavy traffic, ETAs are hopelessly optimistic and misleading.

THE REASONING BEHIND THE CHOICE OF AN ALTERNATIVE TO AN EXCESSIVELY LONG ROUTE

There are a number of factors that should be taken into account when considering an alternative to the proposed satnav route in figure 12:

- The time of the day. Peak traffic congestion occurs in the morning and evening.
- The direction of flow of traffic in and out of a city at peak times, into the city in the mornings, and out in the evenings.
- Known congested roads, and
- Congestion discovered on the day of travel.

The satnav-generated route shown in figure 12 might be appropriate in certain circumstances. Perhaps widespread congestion has been discovered with the more direct route, in which case the longer route might be chosen. However, in general the more direct route is likely to be favoured despite the ETAs, which are, as previously mentioned, misleading.

WHY THE MORE DIRECT ROUTE IS LIKELY TO BE FAVOURED MOST OF THE TIME

The more direct route is likely to be favoured because

- The longer route is excessively long.
- Costs will be much less.
- Less likely to be trapped if traffic congestion is experienced.

HOW TO CORRECT AN EXCESSIVELY LONG ROUTE

Once satnav has displayed the route shown in figure 12, there are a number of ways to correct the route and reduce the distance of travel:

- Exclude the major road leading from the city centre.
- Exclude the orbital road around the city.
- Choose a minor road directly south of the city centre, and select it as an alternative road.

- Allow satnav to generate an alternative or a number of alternatives and then decide on one.

ROUTE FAMILIARISATION

Before setting off on a journey, it is essential to become familiar with the route. Why? If you are not familiar with the route, you will be *blinkered* and dependent on satnav for step-by-step instructions. Your concentration will not be on the road ahead, especially at critical times, and this can cause mistakes, such as a wrong turning or dangerous snap judgements.

How to become familiar with the route:

Examine the route by magnification/reduction and look for all the major roads, which road leads to the next, and in which direction they are heading. You will know the destination town and county from the address, and you may be able to pick out other towns from the overall route display or map detail, depending on the make and model of satnav you are using.

You can also consider the overall distance and estimated time of arrival (ETA) for your route as shown by satnav.

ROUTE FAMILIARISATION SUMMARY

Magnify the route to examine

- Which major road leads to the next.
- The general direction and distance.
- The town nearest to the destination (if this can be discovered).
- Major towns along the route (if satnav detail allows).
- How long the journey will take.

ADVANCED ROUTE PLANNING

Most satnavs allow some form of route adjustment, but detailed, precise routes are not possible with most handheld satnavs. More detailed route planning is possible, however, on a personal computer (PC), the results of which can then be downloaded to a satnav. Some satnav users require more detailed routing with multiple waypoints or stops through which the route must pass. In addition, the TomTom smartphone application (app) version 1.8 allows up to five additional stops or waypoints. One satnav that does allow multiple via or waypoints is the Garmin Nuvi 760. It also allows you to store up to ten of these routes, with multiple destinations in each.

Many PC software products allow detailed route planning, as shown in the table below. (See table 11.) Some of these products are designed for motorbike riders but can be used by anyone; some are particularly good for scenic routes or visiting places of interest. Only one of these products is free.

PC Software for Route Planning

PC software:	Compatible with which satnav?	Countries covered:	Notes:
Tyre	TomTom, Garmin And others	All Countries. (Uses Google Maps). Good for scenic routes and places of interest.	Converts directly to an itn file. It's FREE. www. jamboerma.nl/ net.index.html
Ms Autoroute (UK version of Streets and trips)	Garmin, TomTom and Navagon	European Countries	Use ITNConv. exe to convert it to an itn file.
Streets and Trips 2011 (USA version of above)	Garmin, TomTom and Navagon	US, Canada, Mexico, US Virgin Islands, Puerto Rico	
On route	Garmin, TomTom and Navagon	European Countries	www.on-route. com

PC SOFTWARE FOR ROUTE PLANNING

Mapsource (USA version)	Garmin	US, Alaska and Hawaii	Available from the Garmin website
Mapsource (UK version)	Garmin	UK	Available from the Garmin website

Table 11 compiled from websites cited below.

Tyre: www.tyretotravel.com

Autoroute: www.microsoft.com/uk/autoroute/home.aspx

Streets and Trips: www.microsoft.com/streets

On-route: www.on-route.com

Mapsource (USA): www.garmin.com/us/maps/mapsource

Mapsource (UK): www.garmin.com/garmin/cms/lang/en/uk/maps/tripplanningsoftware/mapsource

Smartphone Apps for Advanced Routing

App	Features	Notes
TomTom app version 1.8	Allows up to five waypoints	www.tomtom.com
Copilot Live Premium	Manipulations of route by touch and drag technique. Identifies places of interest	www.alk.eu.com

Table 12, based on Chipperfield (4.9.11, p. 23).

Other smartphone apps that do not allow advanced routing:

- Navagon Mobilenavigator (www.navagon.com)
- Trafficmaster Companion (www.trafficmaster.com)
- Google Maps with Navigation (www.maps.google.com)
- TomTom with live traffic updates (www.tomtom.com) (Chipperfield, 4.9.11, p. 23)

The smartphone app compared with the dedicated handheld satnav

Now that smartphones are becoming much more popular, it is worth considering their advantages and disadvantages in comparison to dedicated, handheld, satnavs. One of the most authoritative sources of information on the subject is the Which? consumer advice on satnavs, which is found on its website. (See Which? 2012, 'Satnav Reviews: Features Explained'). Here, three categories of satnav are considered and presented as a table:

- Integrated satnavs (supplied with the car)
- Dedicated satnavs
- Apps (downloaded to a smartphone)

The pros and cons of each are described, but what is of interest is that dedicated satnavs are described as more versatile and as providing better performance than smartphone apps. Nevertheless, satnav smartphone apps are becoming increasingly popular.

CONCLUSIONS TO 'ROUTE PLANNING'

The three methods of route manipulation provide a powerful means of altering the original satnav route. These, together with the other techniques described, mean that drivers can develop their own road-navigation skills without the need to waste time sorting out the details of any particular route.

CHAPTER REVIEW

This chapter covered the following points:

How to

- Use an alternative road, often a major parallel road
- Use 'exclude a road'
- Use 'generate an alternate route'
- Use the backflip
- Use the slingshot
- Use the reverse slingshot
- Make a correction to an excessively long satnav route

Sources of information on congestion:

- Local radio
- Feedback from a forward journey
- Major road electronic sign information
- General knowledge of congestion
- Knowledge of the flow of traffic in and out of cities at peak times

Route familiarisation: familiarise yourself with the route, the towns (if possible), major roads with their directions, the total distance, and ETA.

Advanced route planning

- This is possible by downloading to a satnav from a PC.
- Some smartphone apps allow advanced route planning.

CHAPTER 4

Using a Satnav while Driving

REALITY CHECKS AND FOCUS

Assuming you are using a basic-model satnav that does not have live internet traffic updates, then the following advice will prove useful. If, on the other hand, you have a satnav model with live traffic updates, then the following advice will allow you to double-check satnav and to correct it as required during the journey—but not while on the move.

ROUTE FAMILIARISATION

Once you have familiarised yourself with your route and committed it to memory, you can start the journey. Obviously, you will follow satnav visual and verbal directions, but in case of any glitches or confusion, your memorised route should take priority.

When approaching a junction to join a major road, look out for road signs with the correct town, city, or major road designation (e.g., 'Brighton A23' in the UK or 'California Route 66' in the US). Satnav should help with a prompt, the 'next road sign' symbol, although the symbol shown might not always be helpful. Sometimes this shows the next road name, for example, rather than the 'next road sign,' or occasionally there is an error. Attention should be on the road ahead as much as possible until perhaps the later stages of a journey when you may need to pay closer attention to satnav. It is important not to rely too much on a virtual or simulated reality, because this may prove a false sense of security. Any glitches, errors, or misunderstandings can cause major errors of road navigation, hence the need to be familiar with the route and to act on this memory in cases of difficulty. (Satnav should be considered as a useful assistant rather than a master.)

APPLICATION OF ADVANCED DRIVER BEHAVIOUR

The examination of the advanced driver behaviour in the 'Literature Search' suggests that early warning of upcoming events is likely to help with road navigation. Taking a leaf from the advanced driver's book, a satnav user would look to the horizon both on the satnav and in real world to gather information about future turns, junctions, etc. In addition, the next turn symbol can also be consulted, together with the countdown. This advanced notice allows a driver to focus attention on the road ahead at critical times, using the memory of what lies ahead to inform his or her decisions. It releases a driver's attention from satnav to what can be seen through the windscreen. So, instead of relying on satnav when approaching junctions, a driver can rely on memory. The widespread use of this technique could potentially reduce many of the driving errors reported in the survey results in chapter 1. Wrong turnings, near misses, distractions, and veering dangerously all might be reduced.

SUMMARY: GATHERING EARLY WARNING INFORMATION ON THE MOVE

- Look to the horizon on satnav.
- Look to the horizon in the real world.
- Consult the next turn symbol and countdown.
- In the future, it may be possible to safely see beyond the next junction with improved satnav models. (See chapter 6.)

The road immediately ahead, however, must be the focus of attention at critical times, such as approaching junctions or roundabouts. Road sign information and imminent hazards need to be taken into account following negotiation of the correct lane or position on the road.

TACTICS

Congestion can occur at any stage on a journey; it may be sudden, or you may have plenty of notice. If you have had plenty of warning, park at a convenient place and using one of the following methods to plan a way around the congestion.

- Use an alternative road or waypoint.
- Exclude a road (avoid part of route).
- Allow satnav to generate an alternative, provided your satnav is so enabled.

If yor satnav is not enabled with the first two of the three alternatives then you should, at least, be able to use the 'generate an alternative' option which is common to most.

If however, congestion is confronted without warning, first decide if the congestion is likely to be long lasting or temporary. Some congestion fades away quite rapidly and may have to be accepted. If the problem is likely to be prolonged, you might turn off onto a side road, park, and consider the options. When considering which side road to take, first consider the remainder of the route. See figure 13.

HOW TO TURN OFF ROUTE TO AVOID CONGESTION

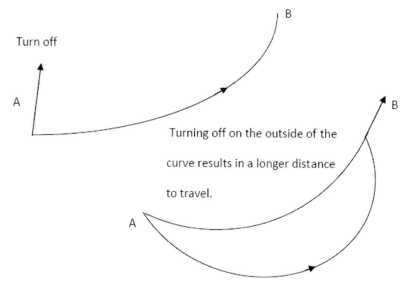

Figure 13.

73

Figure 13 shows how turning off a road inwards from the arch of a curve results in a shorter distance to travel than turning off on the outside of the curve.

Once you have turned off route, you have a choice of allowing automatic rerouting or to park and plan an alternative yourself. If you allow satnav to automatically recalculate your route, ignore satnav's initial attempts to redirect you back onto your original route. Instead, just keep moving away from your original route until a new route is shown.

'AVOID ROADBLOCK' MENU OPTION

'Avoid roadblock' or congestion is another menu feature found on some satnavs. This is a useful feature for avoiding any kind of blockage ahead and may be helpful on some occasions.

HOW TO AVOID TOLL ROADS

Road tolls are becoming ever more prevalent for the modern motorist. Your satnav may have a option that allows you to avoid toll roads when you plan a route. This option will allow either all toll roads or none to be avoided. You may, however, wish to avoid some toll roads but not others.

Consider a route over two hundred miles with a toll near the start and one near the end. A driver may not wish to avoid the toll at the start but want to avoid the one at the end of the journey. How can this be achieved?

A solution might be to take a route initially that avoids all toll roads. Then, after passing beyond the first toll, recalculate the route by choosing the option to avoid toll roads.

How to Avoid Congestion on a Major Road

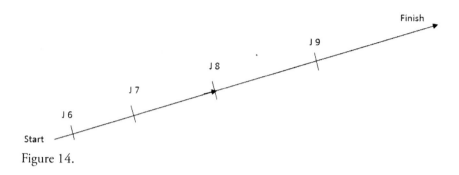

Figure 14.

How to Avoid Congestion on a Major Road

You hear about congestion ahead while travelling on a major road. The congestion is between junctions 8 and 9. (See figure 14.) It may seem like a good idea to avoid the congestion by leaving the major road at junction 7; however, often this is exactly what the majority of other drivers think. So in order to avoid the inevitable secondary congestion, you have to think at least two steps in advance of everyone else.

If this is a long journey, then I would suggest taking a completely different route as soon as possible or at least leave by junction 6. The simplest way to do this is to exclude the major road that you are on. Once you are parallel but beyond the probable congestion, you could return to the original major road. If your satnav does not have the 'exclude a road' option then 'generate an alternative' would produce a similar result.

What advice does this book offer regarding huge lorries being sent down inappropriate narrow lanes?

Firstly, there are some satnavs on the market specifically for trucks. In addition, a standard satnav can be adapted with a software addition. Lastly, a good dedicated street atlas, such as *Philip's Navigator Trucker's Britain*, covers height, width, and weight restrictions. If you are in the US, a good Truckers atlas is mentioned in the Appendices.

Also, if the advice is taken to observe the horizon both on satnav and the real world to establish an early-warning system, this will free a driver to attend to more immediate concerns in the real world when they become necessary. This means road signs like 'Narrow Road' or 'No Entry' will be more likely to be noticed. If satnavs are modified in the way suggested in chapter 6, then it may be possible to see more of the road well ahead on satnav, and this may also help.

When You Reach the Destination

Follow road numbers

Once you reach the final road, check your progress to the destination by following the building numbers along the road; odd numbers are usually on one side and even numbers on the other; however, this is not always the case.

Try the road and town if the postcode does not pinpoint the destination.

If you were unable to confirm the address, or perhaps your destination was the result of a postcode error, try inputting the town and road, and then number on the road. Magnify the results to check it.

Ask locals

If all else fails, try asking responsible people, such as

- Shopkeepers
- Office receptionists
- Security guards
- Police or council officials
- Fuel station staff
- Pedestrians (but ask if they are local first)

Use a map

Sometimes good street maps can be helpful—they even have house numbers along the roads. If you don't have a local map, fuel stations often do.

Asking for directions from local people

Giving and receiving instructions is an important aspect of communication that is particularly relevant to the road navigator. The final leg of a journey can be the most frustrating, if asking for directions results in confusion and misunderstanding. Difficulties include directions which are lengthy and may involve all manners of local landmarks.

What to ask for

- To be pointed in roughly the right direction with an idea of the distance. You can ask someone else much closer to the destination later.
- A road name near the destination.
- A sketch or the route to the destination.
- Written directions.

What not to ask for

It may not be wise to ask for detailed verbal directions to the destination. Anything more than three steps is likely to be forgotten.

Chapter Review

This chapter covered the following points:

Route familiarisation

- Use your memory of the overall route gained prior to the journey.

Gather early warning information on the move

- Look to the horizon on satnav.
- Look to the horizon in the real world.
- Consult the next turn symbol and countdown.
- In the future, it may be possible to safely see beyond the next junction.

Tactics

If you encounter congestion, use tactics to work around it, but always park before adjusting satnav. The following tactics may be used:

- Turn inwards on the concave side of your route and allow automatic rerouting.
- Use 'alternative road.'
- Use 'exclude a road.'
- Use 'generate an alternative.'

At the destination

- Follow the numbers of buildings up or down the road.
- Try the road and town if the postcode does not pinpoint the destination.
- Ask locals for information.
- Use a local map.

CHAPTER 5

Review of a High-specification Satnav with Live Traffic Updates

This review concerns the TomTom Go Live 1000 and attempts to answer a question: does this satnav do what is expected of it? The points below provide the expectations. Firstly, this model is priced at over two hundred pounds in the UK and has a yearly tariff for the traffic information. For this price, you also get the Google search facility to find local company addresses and weather information.

Advantages* (This is not a complete list of the attributes of this satnav.)

1. A powerful processor. Quick to plan routes and redirections.
2. A clear, glasslike screen.
3. live internet traffic updates and quick updates of this information every three minutes. The display of congestion is shown on the overall display as well as the on-route display.
4. Live traffic congestion information is also shown as a bar graph to the right of the screen on the on-route screen.
5. Improved map detail with more town names.
6. Voice activation when required.
7. Incorporates most of the features of previous models and builds on them.
8. Shows the destination once you have input an address to allow you to check it before the route is planned.
9. Shows the 'next road sign' at the top of the screen.
10. Shows the next turn arrow and a countdown distance as a display at the bottom middle of the screen.

11. Slim body shape.
12. If congestion is encountered during the journey, satnav will reroute (if the new route is accepted by the user).
13. Allows Google search for company name destinations, which the satnav will accept for routing.
14. Allows up to three waypoints when route planning.
15. Allows an increased range to be seen on the 2D on-route display.

*Adapted from the TomTom Go Live 1000 Europe Product Specification and Reference Guide. (See www.tomtom.com.)

DISADVANTAGES: DOES TOMTOM GO LIVE 1000 FULFIL EXPECTATIONS?

1. The screen: Although the screen is very clear and displays colour well, it is not very good as a touch-screen interface. Compared to previous TomTom models, this screen is extremely sensitive and yet the screen thickness does not always allow for accurate selection (i.e., the screen seems to be too thick). The result is that you either input digits very slowly and carefully or the process becomes fiddly and often means the wrong item is selected. (Previous TomTom models do not suffer from this.)
2. Traffic updates: A very good system for main roads, it's not quite so good for minor roads. I have been misled a number of times into thinking I could get around congestion on a major road only to find the minor roads around the congestion were just as bad but not shown as such on the satnav display. However, this is not always the case, and often even minor roads are well represented. The congestion shown on the overall display is very useful; this allows alternative routes to be considered. Also, if a number of alternative routes are already known, then satnav can be used as a 'congestion radar' if left on overall display, allowing the navigator to negotiate his or her own route through the congestion. This is ideal for commuters but remember not to adjust satnav while driving.
3. Map detail: The improved map detail is very good, allowing more towns to be seen, but even more detail would be needed to match that of a typical road atlas.

4. Voice activation: It is nice to see this as part of a satnav because eventually it will be perfected. However, it is not perfect yet. Places and road names are not always recognised even on a second or third attempt.

5. The destination: The close-up view of the destination shown by this satnav, once a route has been planned, is to be applauded and confirms my assertion that the destination, as found by satnav, must be checked before setting off on a journey. As an attempt at preventing the problems of finding a wrong destination, it fails to solve the problem fully. A static display of the destination found is displayed, and if the road name can be seen then this would constitute a confirmation. But the actual road name does not always appear on the road shown. In such circumstances, the user is left looking at an unnamed road and, unless familiar with the area, will have no idea if it is correct or not; a close-up view of the destination like this can be misleading. It is far better to equip the user with the knowledge to check the destination by magnification. He or she can then search along the road to find the road name and often the road number. In addition, the overall area and direction of the route can be checked.

6. 'Next road sign': The display of the 'next road sign' information at the top left of the screen is good when it is accurate and when it actually matches the road sign to look for in the real world. The 'next road sign' symbol follows from the tradition of route itinerary practice, which has been identified as done well in the Literature Search by the AA with its Route planner. (See chapter 1.) However, I am not convinced the 'next road sign' information for this satnav is as good as it might be. (Note: many other satnavs deal with the issue in the same way and my comments are not confined to this model alone).

Usually the correct main road designation is shown, but sometimes the correct main road is shown but the wrong town, leaving the driver confused. (Note: this does not occur often.) Alternatively, the next road *name* is displayed, but because it is a minor road, no road directional sign in the real world shows it. This happens frequently and is referred to in the reference guide as normal practice. (See the TomTom website.)

I wonder sometimes if designers have lost their way. Do designers realise why the 'next road sign' information is important? Why would a driver want to know the name of the next minor road? It's unlikely drivers will catch a glimpse of the next minor road name sign in the real world, and even if they manage to do this, it is unlikely to help them with road navigation. So why display it?

7. Next turn indicator at bottom middle of the screen: I do not see any real need for any of the three displays of compressed information at the base of the screen. The first shows the vehicles speed and indicates the speed limit, the middle shows an arrow with a countdown distance to the next turn, and the third shows the estimated time of arrival (ETA) together with the total time for the journey. I would much rather see just the road ahead simulation (on-route) display together with the 'next road sign' and nothing else. An improvement would be to substitute the next turn information from the bottom of the screen for the 'next road sign' symbol, at the top of the screen, when no road sign in the real world exists for the next turn. So the 'next road sign' would appear when a real road sign is upcoming, and the next turn arrow would show instead as an alternative when travelling through minor roads, for example. (Or the road sign plus next turn symbol could be shown together.)

8. Rerouting around congestion while on-route: This facility works well. The fact the overall route is shown to the user for acceptance is good because it means the driver decides if the route is acceptable, rather than satnav. Note: a new route is not always displayed, particularly on minor roads. This means satnav is not providing the driver with the information necessary to make a decision, yet it asks the driver to decide if the new route is to be chosen—a rather confusing situation.

9. Traffic congestion direction is perhaps not displayed as well as it might be on the overall route display. White dots appear within the red or yellow thick lines that represents heavy traffic. It is not easy to see the direction these dots are moving, and this can be misleading. Perhaps stripes rather than dots would be clearer.

10. Increased range on the 2D on-route display. This is an improvement on previous models because when the 2D on-route display is magnified, it remains on the magnification setting adopted as you travel. This is not the case with the 3D display. See chapter 6 for more detail on this and why it is significant.

Conclusion

The TomTom Go Live 1000 is very useful, particularly for the live traffic function. When left as an overall display, this satnav allows drivers to 'see' congestion all around them. This feature alone means this model is worth the price of purchase. Beyond this, the fiddly input screen means it would arguably be more suitable for longer journeys rather than multiple short-run destinations every day.

Chapter Review

This chapter covered the following points:

Drawbacks of TomTom Go Live 1000

- The screen can be fiddly and difficult to use as an interface.
- Live internet traffic updates are generally good but seem not to be as good with minor roads.
- Voice activation: this seems not as good as might be expected.
- Confirming the destination as correct: a close-up, static view of the destination does not always reveal the name of the target road, and when this is the case, the destination cannot be confirmed.
- 'Next road sign' information: when no road sign for the next turn exists in the real world, this satnav shows the next road name, and this is not considered particularly helpful.
- The three displays of condensed information at the bottom of the on-route screen are not considered essential at this location and may be better placed elsewhere, leaving more space for the primary function to show as much of the road ahead as possible.
- Rerouting around congestion: The new route is not always displayed. This means the user sometimes is cut out of the loop

and testifies to my point about disempowering the user. (See the next chapter.)

- The display of the direction of traffic congestion—white dots—cannot easily be seen on the overall display, and this can be misleading.

CHAPTER 6

Evaluation of the Satnav Concept

There has to be something wrong with our satnavs today! Something must be wrong with a device that causes so much havoc and despair amongst drivers, as reported in the survey results in chapter 1. Wrong turnings, swerves, near misses, and confusion face drivers who navigate the road network with a satnav. In addition, many drivers report ending up at the wrong destination. Some of these errors are perhaps due to inexperience, but could it be that the satnav itself is a flawed design?

Developing expertise with a satnav means living with and getting to know satnav intimately, and in so doing, the advantages of satnav can be fully appreciated. But the limitations become all too apparent as well.

In this chapter, it is argued the current approach to satnav design may be flawed not because of some technicality, but because the assumptions upon which the design rests may be misconceived. In particular, there is a suspicion that satnavs in general show too little of the road ahead. One way to establish if this is correct is to road-test a satnav of the suggested improved design—see the WBT approach—and then judge this against driving experience with the current design.

THE CURRENT APPROACH TO SATNAV DESIGN: JUST IN TIME (JIT)

The current approach to satnav design is to provide the driver with information which might be termed 'just in time' to be useful. This approach works alongside the tendency to transform real-life information into a condensed, sanitized form.

JIT APPROACH

REALITY

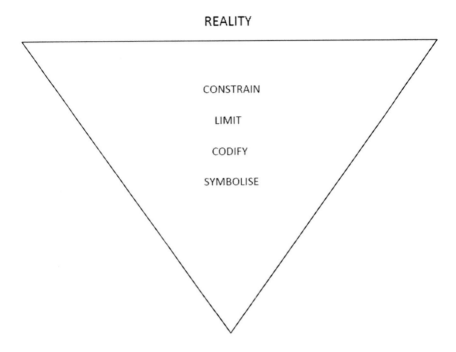

CONSTRAIN

LIMIT

CODIFY

SYMBOLISE

SATNAV CONDENSED SANITIZED REPRESENTATION OF REALITY

Figure 15.

JIT APPROACH: ASSUMPTIONS ABOUT THE SATNAV USER

On this view—see figure 15—the satnav user is disempowered and control is kept with satnav. To be fair, a driver who is new to using a satnav perhaps needs to be in this position, but what about a more experienced user?

Reality is condensed, on this view, into a small screen representation to be followed step by step and presented with other symbolic information. Also, there is a suspicion the distance shown of the road ahead may be too short. If it is too short, this might leave a driver with little warning of events and may make drivers attend to satnav at critical times when they should be looking at the road. For some motorists, just-in-time information might be just-too-late! In particular, when approaching junctions, satnav magnifies the junction (the 2D view shows this well) just at the time when the experienced driver is likely to want to find out what's beyond the junction. A close-up view of a junction is irrelevant to the driver, because when approaching a junction, the driver should be doing two things: watching for the appropriate road signs and positioning the vehicle appropriately. Does the traditional map or atlas user require close-up views of junctions? Yet map readers manage to get from A to B. How do they manage? There may even be a case to reduce the scale of the on-route display when approaching junctions rather than magnify it. Field trials could establish whether this would be better than the current approach.

INPUTTING A POSTCODE OR ADDRESS

Again, on the JIT view, control is kept with satnav. The user is supposed to input a postcode or address and then, I assume, simply follow satnav wherever it leads. For example, the TomTom user guide for a basic model in 2009 suggests inputting an address, and then satnav will do the rest (i.e., plan a route for you).

RANGE

Perhaps it's too difficult to design a satnav with a longer range, or perhaps it is not considered necessary. Could the reason for the next turn symbol and arrow be an attempt to compensate for this issue? If it is, then I wonder if it works. Also, another symbol to represent reality is a further step away from reality and no substitute, in my opinion, for the direct map view. Here is an example of the sort of information that should be in a user guide (i.e., what the next turn symbol represents—together with the countdown—and why it is useful).

When driving, I want quick, simple, and easy-to-understand information. In addition, I want as few representations of reality as possible. The next turn information might be appropriate when no road sign in the real world exists for the next turn. On the other hand, next turn information might be useful in addition to 'next road sign' information displayed in the same place at the top of the screen (but at a small scale), if three times the range on the road cannot be displayed. Note: some makes of satnav already position this symbol at the top of the screen. This seems better than the bottom of the screen.

A Possible New Approach: Well Before Time (WBT)

Instead of providing drivers with information which is just in time, this suggested new approach advocates providing information well in advance, taking a leaf from the advanced driver's book. The Well-Before-Time (WBT) approach allows the driver to see farther ahead on the road, beyond the current range on satnav. Then, when it really matters near junctions or turns, attention can be on the road in the real world. Also, this approach accepts that road navigation with a road atlas has never presented the problems satnav users have to face when trying to navigate roads.

The atlas user's approach suffered because the driver could not hold enough information in his memory but was good because it allowed the driver the freedom to look at the road ahead in the real world. Presumably, satnav cannot display three times the range all of the time, because when approaching junctions where the road turns back on itself, for example, three times of none route map would be displayed ahead rather than the route turning backwards. A simple solution to this might be to use the map-reduction button. Reducing the scale of the on-route view will allow more of the road ahead to be seen. However, tampering with satnav while driving is dangerous. A compromise might be to position a second reduction button on the steering wheel, allowing safe and easy operation. More on this follows. See 'Compromise solution?'

Well Before Time (WBT)

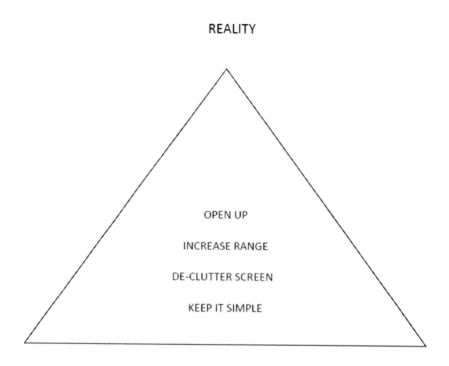

REALITY

OPEN UP

INCREASE RANGE

DE-CLUTTER SCREEN

KEEP IT SIMPLE

SATNAV HAS BETTER 'FIT' WITH DRIVERS NEEDS

Figure 16.

WBT APPROACH: ASSUMPTIONS ABOUT THE SATNAV USER

On this view, see figure 16. The driver is empowered. Here, the driver is allowed to control which features appear on the screen. He or she can remove or turn off beeps, whistles, and other symbolic information at will. Only the map, route, and 'next road sign' symbol would be a basic requirement. This view assumes the user is experienced and is well informed.

Now that satnav has had time to mature as a product, perhaps it is time to clarify the drivers' needs rather than to endlessly add new features. Such a list might be as follows:

Possible drivers' needs

1. Overall, map view of congestion information and on-route congestion information.
2. Predictive congestion information on overall display and on-route display. (See below.)
3. Early warning for upcoming events, such as junctions, by allowing increased range to be shown safely together with a user guide explanation of the need for it.
4. 'Next road sign' and next turn information (if a longer range is not possible).
5. To see what's beyond the next junction rather than a close-up of the junction.
6. To be able to switch off (disable) all extraneous features other than the road view ahead and 'next road sign' or turn information.

Compromise solution?

It may well be that satnav cannot easily be redesigned to show more of the road ahead and would perhaps be uneconomic. A compromise solution might be as follows:

- The reduction feature might have dual activation. The second point of control could be a button where the steering wheel crossbar meets the steering wheel so that the thumb of the driver can operate this function more safely while driving. A Blue Tooth or other wireless connection might be possible. The reduction function would allow the driver to safely see a longer-range view of the road ahead when required.

User guide

- The user guide could be developed to provide drivers with guidance on how to use a satnav while driving; perhaps the principles of using a satnav from this book might be used together with an explanation about how to gather information well in advance and why. It amazes me how a device, used for road navigation in a vehicle, can be sold with nothing to explain how to use it while driving! Apologies to any manufacturer who provides such information, but I haven't come across anything to date.

- The user guide could also include a procedure to confirm the destination as correct. (See the conclusion to the book.) This procedure allows the user to know where satnav will take him or her and to know if this is the correct destination *before* the journey begins.

PREDICTIVE TRAFFIC CONGESTION INFORMATION

A live internet traffic satnav model might be improved with the addition of a predictive congestion feature. The traffic congestion can be very different half an hour after the start of a journey compared to the congestion shown when the route was originally planned, especially if starting a journey just before the height of the peak-time traffic. This is a problem because you can be stuck in traffic which wasn't showing when the route was planned. What is needed, therefore, is a facility to plan a route as though it was half an hour or an hour forward in time. How can this be done? This can be simulated based on historical data, which can be adjusted to allow for anomalies and congestion patterns.

Simulated traffic congestion patterns for peak times adjusted for

- Friday afternoons
- Monday mornings
- Saturdays
- Sundays
- Regular holidays
- School holidays, etc.

A whole year can be simulated in this way, and this can be adjusted each year for differences.

All that would be then required is two additional features on the menu: one for predicted congestion in half an hour and a second for predicted congestion in an hour. I doubt whether more than these two time intervals would be useful. The half-hour prediction would be useful for the commuter and the hour prediction might be useful for someone taking a longer journey. Then route planning should be made possible through this predicted traffic congestion. It may be useful to have a facility to save this route as well.

NEXT TURN SYMBOL

Firstly, if more of the road ahead could be seen, there would be little need for this symbol. However, if in future this symbol is retained, then perhaps consideration could be made to simplifying it. As already suggested, the symbol is more likely taken note of if it appears at the top of the screen rather than the bottom, and perhaps it might be translucent. A further possible improvement might be to replace the current 'distance to turn' countdown shown in yards to a simpler countdown from 10 to 1. Each unit, on this new approach, might represent fifty yards. The driver would then see a less complex countdown to the next junction, which satnav users would soon get use to. No measurements in yards would be needed, as the driver would soon become familiar with this simple countdown. This would be preferable to trying to imagine how far 450 yards might be while trying to drive at the same time. The symbol designation might be simply 'countdown.' Also, I question the need to inform drivers of the next turning if it is twenty miles ahead on a motorway, for example.

SUGGESTIONS FOR A POSSIBLE REDESIGN OF SATNAV

1. Provide a facility to show three times the range.
2. Display the 'next road sign' information at top of the screen.
3. Display next turn symbol, at a smaller scale, also at the top of the screen—perhaps a translucent symbol. A simpler 10-to-1 countdown.
4. Review magnification of junctions, and consider little or no magnification or a reduction instead.
5. Most other features might be optional so that the driver can decide to use them or not.
6. The estimated time of arrival and time to destination could be on the overall display or as a menu option, or they might take up less screen area.
7. A traffic congestion overall display is useful in itself; perhaps a second satnav or split screen might be useful.

8. Improve map detail even more than on the TomTom Go Live 1000, although this is good.
9. A predictive traffic congestion capability allowing routing through this.
10. An improved user guide to include something like the principles of road navigation with a satnav and a procedure to confirm the destination as correct.
11. Improve the next turn symbol.

Perhaps satnavs or smartphone apps will gradually evolve into something better fitted to drivers' needs, or perhaps a dedicated satnav for experienced users will emerge. Further research and development based partly on surveys of experienced drivers' views and satnav users might prove fruitful.

Chapter Review

This chapter covered the following points:

- It is argued that the current approach to satnav design tends to keep control with satnav, presenting drivers with just-in-time information.
- Range: the distance shown of the road ahead on satnav seems short. This may be particularly significant when approaching junctions.
- A redesign of satnav might remedy the above problems, if they are accepted as such.
- Pointers are suggested for further research and development.

CONCLUSION

This book allows a driver to cut down on errors when using a satnav. It means more certainty that the correct destination will be reached. It also means that many of the difficulties and problems experienced when using a satnav can be mitigated.

The truth is the simple act of using a satnav is not quite as simple as first it appears; in fact, as this book shows, it is fraught with difficulties and confusion. The satnav user is urged to cut through the 'fog' surrounding its operation with tried and tested procedures that cut out many of the errors that can occur.

The identification of the satnav 'mindset' problem allows drivers to think outside the box when planning routes.

In addition, the process of considering the difficulties and issues that surround the use of a satnav should put drivers in a good position from which to learn and to develop beyond the limits of this book.

The formulation of the principles of road navigation with a satnav provides a firm foundation for all who own or wish to own a satnav to gain control and develop skill. The described route-planning techniques should allow routes to more closely match user requirements, and pointers have been provided for those who want advanced routing.

Lastly, an argument is made for the re-examination of drivers' needs and to get back to basics with satnav design.

Four major conclusions are drawn from this examination of the satnav

1. Not enough advice is provided for the satnav user, particularly on how to use a satnav while driving.
2. There is a need for a greater understanding of the satnav and how to use it effectively.
3. Using a satnav is a skill that requires both understanding and practical application over time; it is made more complex because it must overlay the skill of driving.
4. It may be possible to improve the design of satnav to provide a better fit with drivers' needs.

In addition, 'the principles of road navigation with a satnav' together with 'how to confirm a destination as correct' provide quick reference guides for satnav users and form part of the conclusions to the book, as follows.

Day-to-Day Quick Reference:
The Principles of Road Navigation
with a Satnav

BEFORE YOU EMBARK ON A JOURNEY, ALWAYS

- **Confirm** your destination. Magnify the satnav-found location and compare with the address. You must be sure the destination is correct before starting off.
- **Plan your route.** Make improvements to the satnav-generated route, to develop your own navigational skills.
- **Familiarise** yourself with your route: the main roads, the main towns (when these can be easily discovered), the main directions of the route, and, if possible, the closest town to your destination.

This process may take several minutes but can save a considerable amount of time on the journey.

WHEN DRIVING

- **Horizon** observation both on satnav and in the real world, to establish an early-warning system for upcoming events and to allow you to attend to reality for short-range concerns at critical times, such as junctions. Also, consult the next turn symbol.
- **Anticipate** future events by positioning appropriately on the road and/or seeking a suitable lane.
- **Road** observation at critical times. Look to the road immediately ahead for road signs (not just directional signs) at critical times, such as approaching junctions.

Remember **C P F / H A R** as the six principles of road navigation with a satnav.

Note: Observation of the road is a continuous process of switching from long—to short-range and back again to gather information.

Procedure to Confirm the Destination Is Correct for the UK

Most people use the postcode to input into satnav. The following procedure is therefore suitable:

How to eliminate the majority of errors when locating the destination

- **Check that the postcode is replicated** exactly as input.
- Whether this is correct or not, **magnify the destination** and check that **the road corresponds** to the road in the address. (Note: the road may be nearby and therefore the destination could be accepted).

If the destination road is not correct,

- **Input the town** (and check the county, where possible) **then road,** and then number on the road instead of the postcode.
- **Magnify the destination** and check that the road is correct.

If the destination road still does not correspond to the road in the address,

- **Look up the address in a street atlas.** If the destination road is shown, then find a side road nearby and input this into satnav instead.

If you cannot find the destination on a map,

- **Cross-check with another source of the address.**

If you haven't another source of information on the address, then refer to the person who provided the address before you set off.

Procedure to Confirm the Destination Is Correct for the United States

How to eliminate the majority of errors when locating the destination

- **Check that the zip code is replicated** exactly as input.
- **Input the town, then road, and then number on the road.**
- **Magnify the destination** and check that the road found corresponds to the road in the address.

If the destination road is not correct,

- Check the roads near the location. If none of these are the correct road, then look up the address in a street atlas. If the destination road is shown, then find a side road nearby and input this into satnav instead.

If you cannot find the destination in an atlas, cross-check with another source of the address.

If you haven't another source of information on the address, then refer to the person who provided the address before you set off.

Postcode Template for the UK

For the UK, the following template is designed to reduce the confusion regarding where letters or numbers are positioned within the postcode. Such a template for the UK could be incorporated into a satnav directly below or above the place where digits are input, and it might look like that shown in chart 7.

Postcode Template for the UK

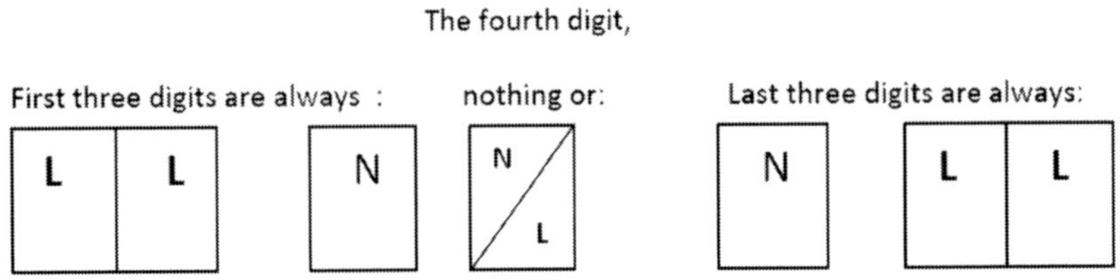

The fourth digit,

First three digits are always :   nothing or: Last three digits are always:

| L | L | | N |

| N |
| L |

| N | | L | L |

Note: L represents a letter, N represents a number and N/L could be either or nothing.

Chart 7.

Justification of the Principles of Road Navigation

To conclude, there are six main points to emerge from the book, which have been termed the principles of road navigation with a satnav. They are shown in the conclusion as a quick reference section, and the following justification is offered for each.

1. The destination must be confirmed.

Why?

> You have to know exactly where you are going before you set off. Simply inputting an address into satnav and then setting off is asking for trouble.
>
> You also need to check that the location found by satnav corresponds to the address, or you cannot be sure you will reach the correct destination.

2. The route should be planned or modified by the user.

Why?

To reach the destination more quickly.
To avoid congestion.
To curb the excesses of satnav (wasted time or fuel), and
To develop your own navigational skills and road network knowledge.

3. Familiarise yourself with the route

Why?

> During a journey, many difficulties may be encountered: distractions, glitches, lost satellite reception, and misunderstandings to name a few. To avoid a longer-than-expected journey, you must be in a position to make instant decisions.

4. Horizon observation

> Observe the road well ahead on satnav, if possible. But if the range doesn't allow, then observe the symbol for the next turn and become familiar with the countdown, (if one is incorporated with the symbol). The actual road ahead may also be observed as far as the view of the road allows. If satnav is improved, it may be possible to safely view the road ahead on satnav much further than at present, and this might negate the need for the next turn symbol.

Why?

> Long-range observation is particularly important to gain advanced warning of upcoming events, such as turns and junctions. Also, knowing what will happen beyond the next junction helps when deciding lane position. (This is difficult at present because the range ahead, on satnav, shortens as junctions are approached.) Long-range observation allows appropriate lane or position on the road to be adopted in good time. It might also prevent a lot of the problems drivers encounter, particularly when beginning to use a satnav.

> **A note on why it is important to know what's beyond the next junction.**

> Consider the example of two lanes of traffic approaching a junction where you want to turn right. Soon after the junction there is another turn you wish to take, this time to the left. As

you approach the first junction your get into the right hand lane and satnav magnifies the junction so you are *blinkered* to what is beyond the first junction. After turning right you find you are now in the wrong lane for the next left turning and on the inside of you is a continuous line of traffic. Other similar examples could be imagined.

5. Anticipate

Being prepared for upcoming events means much more confident driving, and getting into the correct lane is part of this.

Why?

If you do not get into the correct lane or position on the road, then late turns or cutting up other drivers might be a temptation. Or you may be forced to take a wrong turning.

6. Road observation

When approaching junctions, for example, observation should be focused in the real world: the road ahead, road signs and not satnav. Two acts of memory will help: route familiarisation prior to the journey and short-term memory of your observation of the horizon both on satnav and the road ahead. This will allow you the mental freedom to observe the road without the need to consult anything else. It follows, therefore, that the lead up to a junction is a critical time to concentrate on nothing but driving and navigation.

Why?

It is vital to attend to the road ahead at critical times because you might miss a no-entry sign, red traffic light, narrow road sign or traffic coming from another direction, etc.

APPENDICES

Suggested Levels of Skill
When Using a Satnav

Like driving, using a satnav is a skill which cannot be learned by using the device a couple of times. It is a complex activity, because it overlays the skill of driving and has to be woven into the driving experience. The following levels are not prescriptive and are provided only to illustrate the difference between a beginner and an experienced satnav user.

Level 1.

You have used satnav on a few journeys and can

1. Input an address or postcode and check it is replicated as entered.
2. Follow satnav instructions as you travel.

Level 2.

You have used satnav on an almost daily basis for many journeys over half a year. You can

1. Input an address or postcode and check it is replicated as entered.
2. Confirm the destination found by satnav matches the road in the address.
3. Plan a number of alternatives before deciding on a final route.
4. Familiarise yourself with the route before starting the journey.

5. Keep attention on reality—the road ahead—during the journey, relying on your memory of the route as well as following satnav directions.

Level 3.

You have used satnav on an almost daily basis for numerous journeys over a year. You can

1. Input an address or postcode and check it is replicated as entered.
2. Confirm the destination found by satnav matches the road in the address by magnification.
3. Plan a number of alternatives before deciding on a final route.
4. Familiarise yourself with the route before starting the journey.
5. Use a number of tactics during a journey to avoid congestion as appropriate.
6. View the horizon on satnav, the next turn arrow, as well as the road well ahead to gather early warning information allowing anticipation and the appropriate lane to be adopted.
7. Attend to the road, not satnav, immediately ahead when approaching junctions. You are relying on your *memory* of route familiarisation and horizon observation.
8. Use a range of sources of information on congestion to inform your decisions.
9. Source local knowledge quickly and effectively near the end of your journey if you have not found the exact destination.

REFERENCES

Eyre, E. C. (1982). *Mastering Basic Management*. London: Palgrave Macmillan.

Philip's Navigator Trucker's Britain. London: Philips (Octopus), 2009.

'UK Postcodes': The h2g2 website is owned by Not Panicking Ltd. http://h2g2.com/dna/h2g2/alabaster/A12338615.com.

TomTom One XL User Guide. Netherlands: TomTom, 2009.

Highways Agency website: www.highways.gov.uk.

Collin's *Sat Nav Buddy*. London: Collins/Harper Collins, 2009.

'TomTom Route Planner': www.tomtom.com.

'AA Route Planner': www.theaa.com/route-planner/index.jsp

Survey evidence: The Best In-Car Device, 27.12.2008: www.theaa.com/public_affairs-panel/aa-populus-sat-nav-best-device. Retrieved 2010.12.01.

Chipperfield, Ed. *The Sunday Times*, 'The Next Satnav Revolution Is Afoot,' 4.9.11.

Transport for London: 'The knowledge for London taxi drivers': www.tfl.gov.uk.

'How to Become a London Taxi Driver': www.tfl.gov.uk/pco.

Driving for Work: Vehicle Technology. Birmingham, UK: The Royal Society of Prevention of Accidents, www.rospa.com.

Advanced Driving: The Essential Guide. USA: Institute of Advanced Motorists in conjunction with MBI Publishing Company, 2007, www.iam.org.uk.

Cooke, Francis. 'Garmin 'C' Series Menu Structure', 2008, www.aukadia.net/gps/gpsmanual.pdf.

'Which? Computing guides: satnav purchase': www.which.co.uk.

Navman user guides: www.navman.com/au/car-gps-device/user-guides/.

'TomTom Go Live 1000 Europe product specification and the reference guide': www.tomtom.com.

The Complete Drivers Atlas of Britain and Ireland. London: Readers Digest Association LTD, 2004.

Further Reading

USA, Canada, Mexico Motor Carriers Atlas (2012). Rand McNally.

The Occupational Outlook Handbook (2010-11): www.bls.gov/oco/ocos245.htm.

Michelin's website: www.viamichelin.com Route Planner USA

For latest traffic news, AA Roadwatch: 84322 or 843220906 888422 (UK).

Ten-point checklist for using a satnav: www.theaa.com.

Master Atlas of Greater London (2005), Geographers A-Z Map Company (London).

'Questions and answers on satnavs' in 'Which Gadget Questions': www.rac.co.uk.

ADDITIONAL NOTES

3D OR 2D DISPLAY?

The 3D display is an amazing feature of a satnav but may draw the user into reliance on a virtual world rather than dealing directly with reality. My own preference is to use the 2D display. This allows the minor roads on each side of the road to be seen more easily as you travel which is useful when considering alternative routes if you are stuck in slow moving traffic. (See tactics and rerouting.)

The 2D display also helps with learning routes and keeps you in the map-reading mode.

Lastly, if more of the road ahead could be seen with the on-route display, then there would be a clearer view of the horizon or the road at the top of the display. This would allow future turns and junctions and what is beyond the next junction to be seen more easily. This is shown better with the 2D display.

PERSONAL QUALITIES

The satnav user needs to have a number of character strengths to make the most of a satnav for road navigation. First is the ability to analyse routes and evaluate them, then the courage to plan your own course of action and act upon it, and last is the ability to self-assess in order to learn from your own progress. The following qualities are significant:

- Judgement to analyse satnav generated routes
- Courage to plan your own route and follow it
- Ability to act on feedback, and
- Ability to learn from past efforts.

INDEX

A

Advanced Driving ix, 2, 23-4, 28, 105
Advanced route planning xiii, 66, 70
alternative road 16, 47, 52, 57, 59, 61, 65, 70, 73, 78
Asking for directions 77
Automobile Association ix, 1, 8
Avoid congestion 19, 73, 75, 100, 104
Avoid toll roads 74

B

backflip 58-9, 70
Background knowledge xvii
best route 55

C

Collin's Sat Nav Buddy 1, 11, 13, 26, 105
communication x, xvii, 33-8, 41, 45, 77
Confirm xvii-xviii, 12, 25, 33, 39-41, 47, 76, 91, 93, 96-9, 103-4
Confirm a destination as correct 47, 96
confirmation 46, 81
congestion xviii, 6-7, 16, 19, 26, 53, 55, 62, 65, 70, 72-5, 78-80, 82-4, 90-3, 104
Cross-check 98-9

D

Distance shown of the road ahead 86, 93
Distracting 4, 13, 15, 26
Drivers' needs 89-90, 93, 95-6

E

Effective communication xvii, 33-5, 37, 41
Excessively long satnav route 63-4, 70
Exclude a road 9, 48, 52, 62, 70, 73, 75, 78

F

Familiarise 7, 28, 70, 97, 101, 103-4
Fastest route 52-3
feedback 34-5, 37, 41, 70, 107
The four main functions of a satnav 36

G

Gain control 47, 95
Garmin x, 47-9, 67-8, 105
Generate an alternative route 48, 52, 63
Google Maps x, 48-9, 67, 69
Google maps app for a Smartphone 48-9

H

Historical outline 2
How satnav plans routes 53-4, 56

I

input 1, 17, 29, 32-3, 36-42, 45-8,
    59, 79-80, 83, 87, 98-9, 103-4
Institute of Advanced Motorists ix,
    23, 105

J

Just-In-Time Approach 86, 93

K

the Knowledge x, xvi, 2, 7, 18, 27,
    81, 105

L

Levels of skill xvi, 4-5, 103
levers 47
Live internet traffic xiii, 6-7, 15, 27,
    47, 62, 69, 71, 79, 83, 91
London Taxi Driver 2, 18-19, 105
Long-range observation 101
Lorries 75

M

magnification 10, 16, 41, 47-50, 59,
    66, 81, 83, 92, 104
magnify the destination 32-3, 41,
    46, 98-9
menu 1, 9, 16, 47-50, 55, 61, 74,
    91-2, 105

'Mindset' 53, 56, 61, 95

N

Navigational skills 55, 97, 100
Navman xi, 48-9, 105
next road sign 8-9, 25, 71, 79, 81-3,
    87, 89-90, 92
next turn symbol 72, 78, 82, 87,
    92-3, 101

O

observation xvii, 23-4, 97, 101-2,
    104
on-route display 79-80, 83, 87, 90,
    107
Overall display 13, 16, 19, 48,
    79-80, 83-4, 90, 92

P

parallel road 57, 70
PC software for route planning 67
Philip's Navigator Trucker's Britain
    2-3, 14-17, 26-7, 75, 105
Pinpoint an address 32-3, 45
postcode x, 8, 11-12, 26, 29-32, 36,
    38-42, 45-8, 52, 76, 78, 87,
    98-9, 103-4
Pre-input 38-40
Predictive Traffic Congestion
    Information 91
The Principles of Road Navigation
    with a Satnav xi, xvii-xviii, 3, 5,
    7, 9, 11, 13, 15, 17, 19, 21, 93,
    95-7, 99-101
procedure to confirm the destination
    as correct 91, 93

R

range   xvii, 3, 5-6, 22, 63, 80, 83,
    87-8, 90, 92-3, 97, 101, 104
Reality checks   71
Redesign of satnav   92-3
reduction   16, 47-50, 66, 88, 90, 92
Remedial action   21-2, 28
Reverse slingshot   61, 70
Review of a high-specification satnav
    xiii, 79
RoSPA   x, 2, 21, 28, 105
route familiarisation   xvi, 4-5, 7, 47,
    66, 70-1, 77, 102, 104
route manipulation   47, 50, 63, 70
route options   6, 27, 52-3
route planner   ix, 1, 8-10, 25, 62, 81,
    105-6
route planning   xi, xiii, xvi-xvii, 6-8,
    47, 49-50, 52, 66-7, 70, 80, 92
routing   15, 67, 69, 80, 93, 95

S

safety   x, xv, 2, 4, 7, 13, 20-1, 27-8
Satnav app   4, 6
The satnav concept   85
Shortest route   6, 15, 52-3
six principles of road navigation   27, 97
slingshot   59-61, 70
Smartphone   xi, xiii, 4, 6, 47-9, 67,
    69-70, 93
Smartphone app   xi, xiii, 67, 69-70, 93
survey evidence   3, 25, 105

T

TomTom   xi, 6, 8-10, 14, 47-50, 62,
    67, 69, 79-81, 83, 87, 93, 105
TomTom Go Live 1000   xi, 9, 14,
    79-80, 83, 93, 105

V

verification   34-5, 37, 41, 44-5
Verify   37-8, 40, 42-4, 46

W

Well-Before-Time   88
Where errors occur   xvii, 38, 40, 45
Which?   xi, 1, 5-7, 15, 27, 69, 105
Who is ultimately responsible for a
    message?   34

Z

zip code   29, 32-3, 99

Lightning Source UK Ltd.
Milton Keynes UK
UKOW051814170713

213975UK00001B/93/P